40 Short Walks in

KENT

Produced by AA Publishing
© AA Media Limited 2011

Researched and written by
Lindsay Hunt

Additional material and walks
by Rebecca Ford (updated by David
Hancock)

Commissioning Editor: Sandy Draper
Series Management: Sandy Draper
Series Design: Tracey Butler
Copy-editor: Pam Stagg
Proofreader: Chris Bagshaw
Picture Researcher: Liz Stacey
Internal Repro and Image Manipulation:
Sarah Montgomery
Cartography provided by the Mapping
Services Department of AA Publishing
Production: Lorraine Taylor

Published by AA Publishing (a trading name
of AA Media Limited, whose registered office
is Fanum House, Basing View, Basingstoke,
Hampshire RG21 4EA; registered number
06112600)

Enabled by **Ordnance Survey** This product
includes mapping
data licensed from the Ordnance Survey®
with the permission of the Controller of
Her Majesty's Stationery Office. © Crown
Copyright 2011. All rights reserved.
Licence number 100021153.

A04616

978-0-7495-6904-4
978-0-7495-6916-7 (SS)

Colour separation by AA Digital

Printed by Oriental Press

Visit AA Publishing at theAA.com/shop

A CIP catalogue record for this book is
available from the British Library.

Picture credits
The Automobile Association would like
to thank the following photographers,
companies and picture libraries for their
assistance in the preparation of this book.

Abbreviations for the picture credits are as
follows – (t) top; (b) bottom; (c) centre; (l)
left; (r) right; (AA) AA World Travel Library.

3 AA/N Setchfield; 7 AA/N Setchfield; 10
AA/D Forss; 18 AA/P Baker; 30 AA/D Forss;
44 AA/L Noble; 56/7 © TTL Images/Alamy;
82/3 AA/L Noble; 106 AA/D Forss; 118 AA/M
Busselle; 128/9 Maurice Crooks/Alamy; 136/7
© Michael Harris/Alamy.

Every effort has been made to trace the
copyright holders, and we apologise in
advance for any accidental errors. We would
be happy to apply the corrections in the
following edition of this publication.

Opposite: The Saxon Shore Way

40 Short Walks in

KENT

Contents

Walk	Rating	Distance	Page

Rating
Each walk is rated for its relative difficulty compared to the other walks in this book. Walks marked + are likely to be shorter and easier with little total ascent. The hardest walks are marked +++

Walking in Safety
For advice and safety tips see page 144.

Introduction

It's astonishing that so much unspoiled countryside survives so close to London. Britain's south-east corner faces enormous pressures from a relentlessly expanding population. Huge numbers of people live and work here, or pass to and fro on crowded road and rail networks. Now the high-speed rail route is up and running, mainline Kent lies an equidistant 35-minute journey from the capital and from Europe. Yet the Kent Downs and High Weald, totalling a third of the county, are designated Areas of Outstanding Natural Beauty (AONB). Once you leave the highways and take to your feet, you'll soon see why Kent is known as the 'Garden of England'. Many think of Kent's scenery as quintessentially English – perhaps a bit bland or tame. All those chocolate-box villages full of weatherboarded pubs and converted oasthouses, the undulating patchworks of woods, orchards and farmland. True, there are no wild moorlands or mountains here, but Kent's coastline is undeniably spectacular. What landscapes could be more striking and varied than the white cliffs of Dover, the shingle desert of Dungeness or the lonely North Kent marshes?

Rights of Way and Open Access

Kent has over 4,200 miles (6,758km) of public rights of way, plus about 5,600 acres (2,268ha) of recently designated 'open access' countryside (where you don't have to stick to linear paths). Many are age-old trails, following time-honoured trading or droving routes, Roman roads, pilgrimage courses, lines of defence. Some trace the warp and weft of Kent's natural terrain, over chalk downs or sandstone ridges, along cliff tops, coastlines and river valleys. Other paths breathe new life into disused railways and canals, or obsolete industrial sites. There are well-beaten tracks no one could miss and ghostly spoor marks requiring a keen eye for the next waymark. New routes are being established all the time.

Long-distance Footpaths

One of Kent's longest footpaths is the North Downs Way, a superb National Trail extending 153 miles (246km) from Farnham (near Winchester in Hampshire), with a 'shrimp-net' loop at its eastern end linking Canterbury, Dover, Folkestone and Wye.

Other long-distance routes partly covered on the following walks include the Saxon Shore Way, running round most of the Kentish coast; the High Weald Landscape Trail, a scenic path through a rolling patchwork of orchards,

Opposite: Old Oast House in Bethersden

fields and oakwoods; and the Greensand Way, stretching from Surrey's stockbroker belt through some of Kent's most idyllic villages. Riverside walks follow sections of the Darent, Medway and Stour valleys and a tow-path walk leads along the banks of the Royal Military Canal.

Plenty to See Along the Way

Whatever the weather or the time of year, there's always something to catch your interest in Kent. The short walks that follow can be enjoyed simply as undemanding outings through glorious scenery, or vignettes of classic rural charm. But, in addition, each route gives a few glimpses of a rich tapestry of Kentish themes: natural and man-made. As Britain's closest point to Europe, Kent has attracted the attention of invaders and migrants for thousands of years. More than a mere thoroughfare to the rest of Britain, its fertile acres and dry climate have always made it a desirable place to settle. It has a fair claim to be England's oldest county, indeed a former kingdom in its own right. Kent has more listed buildings and archaeological sites, more fortifications and historic houses, and more conservation areas than any other English county. Small wonder then that there is so much to explore.

Using the Book

This collection of 40 walks is easy to use. Use the locator map, see opposite, to select your walk, then turn to the map and directions of your choice. The route of each walk is shown on a map and clear directions help you follow the walk. Each route is accompanied by background information about the walk and area.

INFORMATION PANELS

An information panel for each walk details the total distance, landscape, paths, parking, public toilets and any special conditions that apply, such as restricted access or level of dog friendliness. The minimum time suggested for the walk is for reasonably fit walkers and doesn't allow for stops.

ASCENT AND DIFFICULTY

An indication of the gradients you will encounter is shown by the rating ▲▲▲ (no steep slopes) to ▲▲▲ (several very steep slopes). Walks are also rated for difficulty. Walks marked ✦✦✦ are likely to be shorter and easier with little total ascent. The hardest walks are marked ✦✦✦.

MAPS AND START POINTS

There are 40 maps covering the walks. Some walks have a suggested option in the same area. Each walk has a suggested Ordnance Survey map. The start of each walk is given as a six-figure grid reference prefixed by two letters indicating which 100km square of the National Grid it refers to. You'll find more information on grid references on most Ordnance Survey maps.

CAR PARKING

Many of the car parks suggested are public, but occasionally you may find you have to park on the roadside or in a lay-by. Please be considerate when you leave your car, ensuring that access roads or gates are not blocked and that other vehicles can pass safely.

DOGS

We have tried to give dog owners useful advice about how dog friendly each walk is. Please respect other countryside users. Keep your dog under control, especially around livestock, and obey local bylaws and other dog control notices. Remember, it is against the law to let your dog foul in public areas, especially in villages and towns.

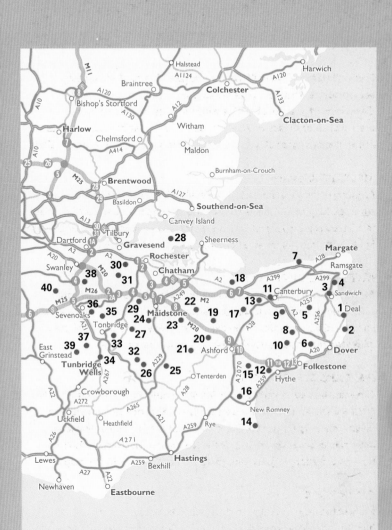

KEY TO WALKING MAPS

--→--	Walk Route	▦	Built-up Area
❶	Route Waypoint	▦	Woodland Area
-- -- --	Adjoining Path	🚻	Toilet
⚡	Viewpoint	🅿	Car Park
•	Place of Interest	🎪	Picnic Area
⌂	Steep Section	)(	Bridge

A WANDER ROUND OLD DEAL

Discover a haven without a harbour on a treacherous bit of coast.

Adjuvate Advenas 'Befriend the stranger' is the welcoming motto of this little seaside town. Its central streets are full of character, a rare survival of an intact Georgian townscape. Middle Street is the most charming and best preserved of Deal's old streets and was Kent's first-ever conservation area. The Georgian houses in this part of town are now carefully gentrified and much sought after. Many would have been the homes of humble boatmen, others the grander houses of wealthy merchants or naval officers.

Deal Castle

A bird's-eye view shows the perfect Tudor rose design of this fortress – an appropriate shape for a castle built by Henry VIII to counter the threat of invasion from Catholic Europe. Deal is the largest and most elaborate of a tripartite series of forts along this stretch of coast (others were built at Walmer and Sandown). Its flat-roofed central tower and surrounding bastions were all heavily armed with the latest artillery. These defences were never put to the test in Tudor times (presumably their very existence was deterrent enough). It wasn't until the Civil War that the castle finally came under siege. By the end of the Napoleonic Wars, Deal castle had had its day as a defensive site, but it served as a military residence until the Second World War. If you look upwards as you approach the main entrance, you'll see five 'murder holes' in the roof, designed for pouring boiling oil or quicklime on any potential intruders.

Deal Pier

Like most of Britain's seaside piers, those built at Deal have taken a pounding from storms and shipping collisions. The first version was only half the intended size (the construction company ran out of cash and had to stop at 250ft/76m). The Victorian pier was demolished during the Second World War (a vessel crashed into it after being struck by a drifting mine in 1940). The present structure dates from the 1950s and has recently had an expensive facelift. A stroll down the pier gives a fine panorama of Deal's seafront. It's a great spot for sea fishing and anglers brave the elements in hopes of a catch.

Opposite: Deal Castle

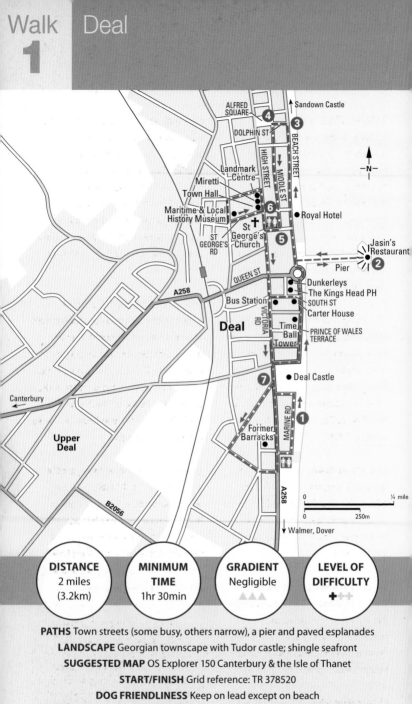

DISTANCE
2 miles
(3.2km)

MINIMUM
TIME
1hr 30min

GRADIENT
Negligible
▲▲▲

LEVEL OF
DIFFICULTY
✚✚✚

PATHS Town streets (some busy, others narrow), a pier and paved esplanades

LANDSCAPE Georgian townscape with Tudor castle; shingle seafront

SUGGESTED MAP OS Explorer 150 Canterbury & the Isle of Thanet

START/FINISH Grid reference: TR 378520

DOG FRIENDLINESS Keep on lead except on beach

PARKING Streetside parking near Deal Castle (free of charge on Marine Road)

PUBLIC TOILETS Marine Road (by the paddling pool), the far end of the pier,
bus station and other central locations

WALK 1 DIRECTIONS

❶ After visiting the castle, head towards the seafront, noticing the fishing boats pulled up on the beach. Turn left along Prince of Wales Terrace, the seafront extension of Victoria Town, a smart residential area of large 19th-century villas built on the site of the old Naval Yard, to your left. A few blocks further along the seafront stands the four-storey Time Ball Tower.

❷ Turn right along the pier and walk to the end for a fine view, then return to the seafront and continue along the promenade (part of the Saxon Shore Way). Nelson caused a frightful scandal when he brought his mistress Emma Hamilton to The Royal Hotel on Beach Street in 1801.

❸ Carry on up the seafront as far as Dolphin Street, then turn left into Alfred Square a block inland. The press gang operated here and smugglers' hiding places are still being found in local houses.

❹ Turn left down Middle Street. Glance right and left down all the side streets, where cobbled courts and passageways create a maze of intimate views and terraces of tightly packed houses crowd the narrow pavements.

❺ Turn right when you reach King Street and walk up to the High Street. Turn right and walk past the parish church of St George, where many naval officers worshipped during the Napoleonic Wars, including Nelson. Beyond it stand the town hall (now the tourist office) and the community arts Landmark Centre. Turn left here up Union Road, left again on West Street and complete the block left again down St George's Road, where you will pass the Maritime and Local History Museum on your left.

❻ Return to the High Street and retrace your steps (look out for Miretti's – see Eating and Drinking). Turn left down South Street to admire a pretty pink-washed house; a plaque explains that from 1762 until her death in 1806, this was the home of Elizabeth Carter, a scholarly woman who became a close friend of Dr Johnson.

❼ Walk down Victoria Road past the inland side of Deal Castle. Turn half right up Gladstone Road, left down North Barrack Road and left again along the Strand to admire some of the fine old barracks buildings here (now converted into elegant housing). Return to your starting point.

🍴 EATING AND DRINKING

On the seafront is The King's Head, a pretty flower-decked pub. Nearby Dunkerleys is a popular seafood restaurant and bar-bistro. At the end of the pier, Jasin's serves family favourites in an award-winning modern building. Miretti's, in the High Street, is an irresistible Italian patisserie and coffee shop.

SURVEYING THE SCENE FROM WALMER CASTLE

Chalk downs and shingle shores near the Lord Warden's residence.

This energetic walk showcases Walmer's assets, starting at its castle and heading to the breezy downland high above the coast. Walmer's more rustic neighbour Kingsdown stands at the northern end of the white cliffs that stretch down to Dover. The return journey is a scenic, gentle stroll along the long shingle beach, where the vegetated shingle is a rare habitat containing some unusual and highly specialised plants. They have to withstand adverse conditions of salt spray and storm damage, as well as low nutrient levels. Look out for sea kale, yellow horned poppy, sea bindweed and vipers bugloss.

Hawkshill Down

The hilly ridge just south of Walmer is an ancient stretch of chalk grassland. Bronze Age remains have been excavated here. It has been used as a military training ground for troops since Deal and Walmer were first fortified in the 16th century and it became an aerodrome in the First World War. A memorial on the walk route commemorates pilots killed in action in France who flew from here. In the Second World War, Hawkshill Down was used as a secret radar base, giving early warning of enemy planes as they headed across the Channel. The land is now a public open space and has amazing views of the across the sea. The Goodwin Sands are clearly visible at low tide.

Walmer Castle

Since 1708, Walmer Castle has been the official residence of the Lord Warden of the Cinque Ports. This ancient office was first established in the 11th century and exerted great power and influence in the defence of the realm. Today it is a purely ceremonial role. The Queen Mother held the title for many years until her death; other famous Lord Wardens have included the Duke of Wellington, Winston Churchill and Henry VIII (before he acceded to the throne). It was Henry who built Walmer Castle in 1540, as part of his chain of Channel artillery defences. Walmer Castle is now an elegant, comfortable home surrounded by beautiful gardens. Wellington's campaign bed and a pair of his boots (the original wellies) are on display in the museum.

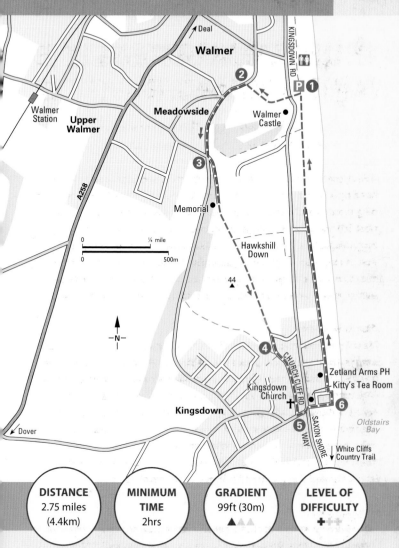

DISTANCE 2.75 miles (4.4km)

MINIMUM TIME 2hrs

GRADIENT 99ft (30m) ▲▲▲

LEVEL OF DIFFICULTY ✚✚✚

PATHS Quiet roads and field or shoreline paths; no stiles **LANDSCAPE** Downland and beach **SUGGESTED MAP** OS Explorer 138 Dover, Folkestone & Hythe **START/FINISH** Grid reference: TR 378503 **DOG FRIENDLINESS** An ideal dog-walking route with lots of scope for exercise; on lead on village roads **PARKING** Car park opposite Walmer Castle (free) **PUBLIC TOILETS** At Granville Road along the Walmer seafront **NOTE** Walking along the shingle beach damages the vegetation – stick to the promenades behind. Occasionally shingle is thrown up in storms and you may have to make a brief detour

WALK 2 DIRECTIONS

1 Cross Kingsdown Road from the car park and walk briefly left towards Walmer Castle. Before you reach it, take the footpath through a gate to your right, walking along a field-edge beside the castle grounds.

2 At the far end, take the gate on to the road and turn left, taking the left-hand fork at the junction (stay on the road here, don't take the footpath). Carry on past Meadowside (a modern complex on your right) as far as Hawkshill Camp Road.

3 Head half-left uphill on the signed footpath 'ED46'. Take the gravel track past an electricity substation into open meadow. Follow the path diagonally to the far corner, following the gappy hedgeline to the right past benches and information boards about the area. You will pass a little lychgate memorial to First World War pilots on your right. Carry on over more fields, descending gently towards Kingsdown village on a clear track. Buildings are visible in the woods ahead. Cross the access drive to a house called Channel Haven, bearing left when the path forks at the end.

4 Go out to Church Cliff road and follow it uphill past houses (Coppice Lodge, El Nido etc), passing a small church to your right at the end.

5 Turn left at the junction, heading down towards the sea. (The Rising Sun pub and Kitty's Tea Rooms lie just to your left here.) Continue over the junction following signs for the Saxon Shore Way towards the beach. At South Road, take the pebble driveway past cottages.

⌖ IN THE AREA

You can follow the Saxon Shore Way south from Kingsdown all the way to Dover, following the white cliffs that erupt behind the shingle beach in a solid wall of chalk. If you're a James Bond fan, you may recall that in *Moonraker* (the book, rather than the film), the evil Sir Hugo Drax's rocket research centre was based here.

---

6 Turn left along the seafront past the Zetland Arms pub. Now simply proceed along the tarmac path, following the shore back past seafront houses and green spaces to the car park by the castle.

🍴 EATING AND DRINKING

Walmer has various cafés and restaurants by the Green and there are tea rooms at the castle. Kingsdown has several pubs too, including the simple but splendidly located Zetland Arms overlooking the beach, which you pass on the walk. Just behind the beach at Kingsdown is Kitty's Tea Room, serving freshly baked cakes, scones and lunches.

A TASTE OF SANDWICH

A gentle trail around this picturesque town
and the Roman remains at Richborough.

As you walk around Sandwich, you can't help but be struck by the town's picturesque appearance, with its half-timbered houses and historic churches. It's hard to imagine these narrow streets echoing with the footsteps of raiders, smugglers and pirates. Yet Sandwich was once the most important port in England – the Dover of its day – and one of the original Cinque Ports.

Strategic Ports

The Cinque Ports was the name given to the confederation of five (later seven) ports on the south-east coast that guarded England in the days before there was an official navy. Hastings, New Romney, Dover, Hythe and Sandwich, together with Rye and Winchelsea, were important fishing and trading centres. This meant they had plenty of men and ships that the King could press into service and in those days Sandwich occupied a strategic position on the coast and was frequently raided by the Danes and the French.

The tradition began with the Saxons and was well established by the time of Edward the Confessor (c1003–1066). By the 13th century, the towns had become so important to England that they were formally granted rights and privileges. These included freedom from taxes and customs duties, some trading concessions and courts. In return, each town had to supply a quota of men and ships whenever required. It provided opportunities for merchants and traders and the Cinque Ports became some of the richest and most powerful centres in Europe.

The quay at Sandwich, now so quiet, would have bustled in those days as men embarked for Europe and ships laden with valuable cargoes were unloaded. Smugglers and pirates operated from here, too, attracted by the rich pickings on offer. All the ports had a violent reputation. However, their power and influence was not to last. A terrible storm in 1287 permanently altered the coastline. The sea began to retreat and the harbour at Sandwich, and other ports, eventually became so choked with silt they could no longer be used. After a permanent navy was established the privileges of the Cinque Ports were revoked and Sandwich sank back into relative obscurity.

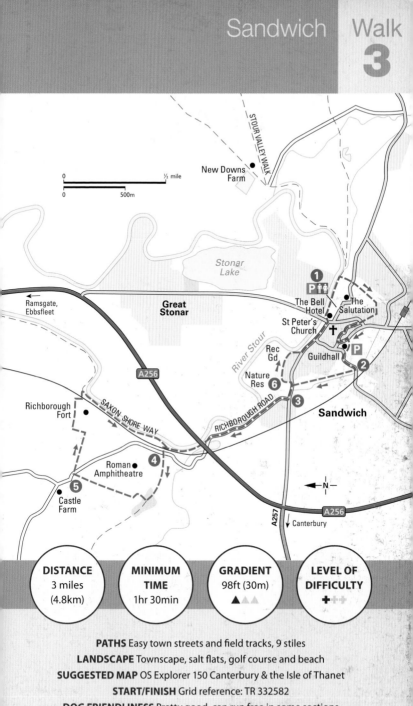

0   ½ mile

0   500m

New Downs Farm

STOUR VALLEY WALK

Stonar Lake

Great Stonar

← Ramsgate, Ebbsfleet

1 P

The Bell Hotel

The Salutation

St Peter's Church

River Stour

Rec Gd

P

Guildhall

2

Nature Res **6**

3

A256

SAXON SHORE WAY

RICHBOROUGH ROAD

Sandwich

Richborough Fort ●

Roman Amphitheatre ●

4

5

Castle Farm

←—N—

A257

A256

↓ Canterbury

| **DISTANCE** 3 miles (4.8km) | **MINIMUM TIME** 1hr 30min | **GRADIENT** 98ft (30m) ▲▲▲ | **LEVEL OF DIFFICULTY** ✚✚✚ |

PATHS Easy town streets and field tracks, 9 stiles
LANDSCAPE Townscape, salt flats, golf course and beach
SUGGESTED MAP OS Explorer 150 Canterbury & the Isle of Thanet
START/FINISH Grid reference: TR 332582
DOG FRIENDLINESS Pretty good, can run free in some sections
PARKING Car park (fee) at Sandwich Quay
PUBLIC TOILETS New Street and The Quay, Sandwich and Sandwich Bay

Opposite: The River Stour at Sandwich

WALK 3 DIRECTIONS

❶ Walk along the river bank away from the town, following the line of the old wall. At a bend in the river, turn right along a tarmac path to the road. Turn right, then left and continue along the path, passing the bowling green. Turn right down steps into Mill Wall Place. At the crossroads, go ahead along King Street, passing St Peter's Church and turn left along No Name Street. Cross New Street to the Guildhall, walk though the car park and up to the Rope Walk, where rope makers used this long, straight area to lay out their ropes.

❷ Turn right and at the road, cross and walk down The Butts. At the main road turn left, cross over and turn right up Richborough Road.

❸ Walk ahead, past a scrapyard, and go through a gate to join a footpath on the right. Follow the track round, under the main road and turn left to cross the railway line via stiles.

❹ Cross the road, go through a kissing gate, then walk across the field to the trees, heading for the third telegraph pole. The path now plunges into the trees. Where it splits, fork right and go through the trees to a stile. Now follow the fence line and turn right at the marker beyond a ditch to reach a gate. Walk up the left-hand field-edge, cross a stile, go through a gate and cross a further stile to the road.

❺ Cross and walk up the track ahead. The Roman Richborough Fort is ahead and the track runs around the fort with expansive views. At the bottom of the track turn right along the end of a garden. Cross the stile and back over the railway, leaving it by another stile. The path now goes immediately right, over a bridge and back beside the river. You will eventually rejoin the road and retrace your steps to the end of Richborough Road where you turn left.

❻ Go left through a kissing gate, pass the Nature Reserve and go round the edge of a recreation ground. Bear right through trees and pass a car park to reach Strand Street and turn left. Go left in front of the Bell Hotel and right past the Barbican.

A WALK ON THE WILD SIDE AT PEGWELL BAY

Retracing historic landing sites
at a coastal nature reserve.

For birders or any lover of wild places, the country park and nature reserve at Pegwell Bay is a wonderful spot. You get a fine view of the bay from the car park if you can bag a shoreline space. If you take to your feet, even for a short distance, you're bound to see dozens of different birds and plants and perhaps even a seal or two. Information boards at intervals tell you what you're looking at and much about the history of the local area. There are picnic benches, too.

Pegwell Bay Country Park

The country park forms part of a much larger National Nature Reserve encompassing the entire bay and extending south of the Stour estuary towards Sandwich. This walk covers only a small section near the car park but even this limited area contains a remarkable range of coastal habitats. Within a few paces you can find saltmarsh, mudflats, rocky shoreline and grassland scrub, supporting a flourishing range of species. There's a fine dune system on the Sandwich side of the bay and a scenic belt of chalk cliffs fringing the Ramsgate headland. It is hard to believe that this glorious wildlife haven was a landfill dump until the late 1970s.

Pegwell is noted for rare orchids and wetland birds. Songbirds, butterflies, lizards and dragonflies inhabit the bushy undergrowth just behind the shoreline. Oystercatchers and redshanks live here all year, while sanderlings, turnstones and plovers spend the winter spuddling about in the bay, returning to their Arctic breeding grounds in summer.

A Viking Longship

At Cliffs End on the north side of Pegwell Bay, you'll find a full-sized replica of a Viking longship parked near the shore. The *Hugin* sailed here from Denmark in 1949 to mark the 1,500th anniversary of the arrival of Hengist and Horsa on Thanet's shores. The commemorative voyage attempted to recreate the conditions those ancient mariners would have experienced. Its 53-man crew carried just one navigational aid on board – a sextant.

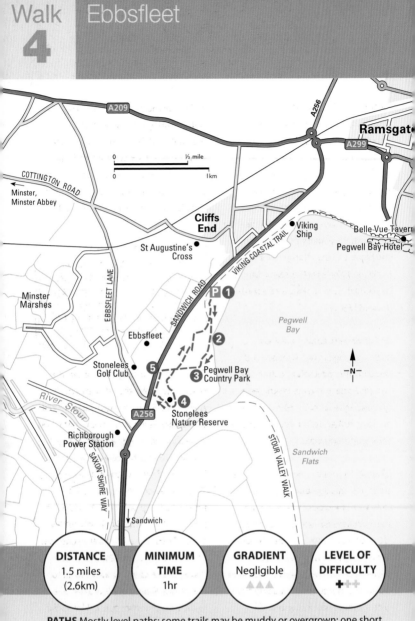

DISTANCE	MINIMUM TIME	GRADIENT	LEVEL OF DIFFICULTY
1.5 miles (2.6km)	1hr	Negligible ▲▲▲	✚✚✚

PATHS Mostly level paths; some trails may be muddy or overgrown; one short flight of steps; no stiles **LANDSCAPE** Varied coastal habitats

SUGGESTED MAP OS Explorer 150 Canterbury & the Isle of Thanet

START/FINISH Grid reference: TR 343635 **DOG FRIENDLINESS** Popular dog-walking spot; keep dogs on leads within the nature reserve **PARKING** At Pegwell Bay (pay-and-display) **PUBLIC TOILETS** Toilets at Pegwell Bay car park being renovated; some near the Viking Ship only open in summer **NOTE** Trails within the reserve may alter from time to time and temporary fencing may be in place

WALK 4 DIRECTIONS

❶ From the car park, follow the shoreline path south, with the sea on your left. Ahead of you to your right are the cooling towers of Richborough Power Station, with more scenic open views across the bay. Waymarked signs on posts indicate the various trails within the reserve; follow the black and blue (long trail) markers. In about 300yds (274m) pass a bird hide to your left, overlooking a crescent-shaped lagoon.

❷ Continue following the main path, bearing to your right around the aprons of tidal saltmarsh on the seaward side (these are restricted areas for nesting or roosting birds). In about another 300yds (274m) reach a line of short concrete pillars.

❸ Head to your left here down some steps and through a kissing gate, following the blue markers through the Stonelees nature reserve, an area of 'dune pasture', with a dense covering of bushes providing cover for lots of different birds. You may find Highland cattle or Exmoor ponies grazing here, with various sections fenced off.

❹ Follow the waymarkers around the path, bearing clockwise. In another 0.25 miles (400m) or so there's a seal viewing point. Once past this, bear right, following the path inland, then right again before you reach a kissing gate leading out towards the road.

> **🐾 ON THE WALK**
>
> A short way inland, beside the Minster road, a 22ft (7m) Celtic cross on a grassy knoll commemorates the momentous encounter of St Augustine with the Kentish King Ethelbert in AD 597.

❺ Follow the inner path back to the pillars, then take the left-hand path and follow the black waymarkers back to the carnpark on the inland path. You can extend this walk along the bay if you wish, a short additional loop takes you around the far side of the car park, ducking inland before you reach a petrol station past brackish saltmarsh lagoons. Alternatively, simply follow the cycle track parallel to the road (part of the Viking Coastal Trail) past the Viking ship and all the way round to the cliffs at Ramsgate. It is a flat, easy walk, though rather spoiled by traffic.

> **🍴 EATING AND DRINKING**
>
> A mobile snack-van turns up at Pegwell Bay car park most days. For something more substantial, head for the popular Belle Vue Tavern on the cliff tops north of the bay (near the turreted Pegwell Bay Hotel). This welcoming Shepherd Neame pub, with terrace tables overlooking the sea, has a wide-ranging menu offering crabcakes, filled panini and interesting main courses, as well as occasional summer barbecues.

AN ENGLISH COUNTRY GARDEN

Through an estate village with a fine garden and Jane Austen associations.

This walk from Goodnestone has plenty of English charm. Many of the houses have a characteristic type of architecture that clearly marks them as part of an estate village. Look at the windows, in quaint Gothic lattice (like the ones on the FitzWalter Arms). Even some newer properties echo this distinctive style.

Along the route, Chillenden's windmill makes a prominent landmark. You can go inside it on summer Sundays or Bank Holidays, though it no longer contains any milling machinery. Dating from 1868, it belongs to a type known as a 'trestle-post' mill, which is turned manually rather than fitted with a fantail. It was one of the last mills ever built to this design in Kent.

Goodnestone Park Gardens

During the summer months, Goodnestone Park Gardens certainly deserve a visit. Romantic, peaceful and varied, they combine the maturity of a long-established estate with the brio of modern design. The original gardens date from the 17th century but have been extensively remodelled and replanted since then, especially since the Second World War when the house was requisitioned for military use. The landscaped park had a fashionable makeover in the 18th century, when Jane Austen's brother Edward married into the FitzWalter family who owned Goodnestone. Jane was a regular guest at the house and Edward's daughter Fanny became one of her favourite correspondents. But the greatest influence on the gardens as they are today is the present owner Margaret FitzWalter (sister of the journalist Lord Deedes – inspiration of *Private Eye's* 'Dear Bill' letters). She has lived at Goodnestone since 1955 and been its most enthusiastic and creative gardener.

Today the gardens cover about 14 acres (5.6ha) and consist of formal and woodland areas with many venerable specimen trees. The oldest part is a walled garden with lots of tender shrubs and climbers. Recent innovations are a spectacular rill garden (water feature), a gravel garden and a box parterre offering a grandstand view over the stately parkland beyond. If you belong to the Royal Horticultural Society you can visit the gardens free of charge (take your membership card).

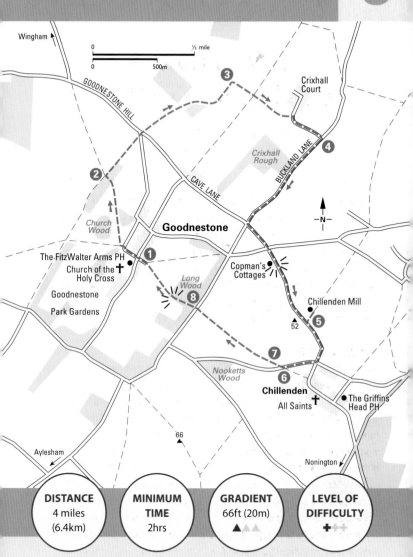

<table>
<tr><th>DISTANCE
4 miles
(6.4km)</th><th>MINIMUM
TIME
2hrs</th><th>GRADIENT
66ft (20m)
▲▲ ▲▲</th><th>LEVEL OF
DIFFICULTY
✛✛ ✛✛</th></tr>
</table>

PATHS Field and woodland paths or quiet country lanes; 3 stiles
LANDSCAPE Woods, fields and historic estate villages
SUGGESTED MAP OS Explorer 150 Canterbury & the Isle of Thanet
START/FINISH Grid reference: TR 255546 **DOG FRIENDLINESS** Can run free
in places; keep under control near stock or on roads; dogs not allowed in
Goodnestone Park Gardens **PARKING** Roadside parking near Goodnestone
church **PUBLIC TOILETS** None on route; try Aylesham railway station otherwise
Canterbury or Sandwich

WALK 5 DIRECTIONS

❶ From the church, walk left up the main street a few paces, and take the footpath sign to the left just past the pub. Walk up School Lane, cross another access road near the top, then take the unmade path ahead, bearing half right where it forks, heading diagonally across a field between stands of woodland (Church Wood and Loverswalk Wood). Continue through the next field to a belt of trees, taking the path through it (look for a marker post) and emerging into a sunken green lane just beyond the wood.

❷ Turn right and take this track beside the field-edge for 500yds (457m) to reach a road junction (Cave Lane and Goodnestone Hill). Cross, taking the bridleway ahead of you, slightly to your right. Follow this track uphill, weaving half right past a patch of woodland after another 400yds (366m).

❸ At the end of the next field, turn right at waymarkers along the hedgeline, crossing an intersecting path. You will soon approach Crixhall Court, half-hidden among trees to your left. When you reach one of its oasthouse outbuildings, follow the arrowed sign to your right, following the avenue of trees down the drive.

❹ When you reach the road (Buckland Lane), turn right and follow it past a patch of woodland called Crixhall Rough (to your right). At the crossroads in about 0.75 miles (1.2km), turn left down Cave Lane, crossing another intersection in 200yds (182m). Carry on passing Copman's Cottages. Chillenden Mill appears to your left.

❺ Continue downhill past the mill, bearing right around a bend. You are now on the edge of Chillenden (take a brief detour here for for the historic Griffins Head pub, which makes regular appearances in gastro-pub guides, at the end of the main street).

❻ Turn right at the crossroads and in 200yds (182m) take the footpath leading half right up a bank.

❼ Carry on half left diagonally across a field, passing Nooketts Wood to your left beyond the lane. Head for a lone poplar at the field margin, where you will find a waymarked stile. Continue straight on over the next field and cross Buckland Lane into Long Wood beyond, a copse of hazel and beech (mind tree roots on the path here).

❽ Keep going downhill through the wood to a stile at the far side, then head diagonally half right across pastureland back to the village. You will see Goodnestone House half right, and the church tower ahead. Bear left by modern houses at the end of the field and take the concrete path out to the main street, where you will emerge by the FitzWalter Arms, an unpretentious local, serving acclaimed food.

A STEEP HIKE ROUND ALKHAM

Valley views and abbey ruins in part of the
Kent Downs Area of Outstanding Natural Beauty.

The pretty village of Alkham lies in a steep-sided chalk valley running
west of Dover. Geology and terrain make it prone to flash flooding – an
underground spring called the Alkham Bourne inundates the area without
warning when the water table reaches a critical level. When it isn't raining,
nothing could be more cheering than this modest English village where
cricket is played on the village green and little seems to have changed here
for centuries. It has a fine 13th-century church and a number of quietly
distinguished houses.

St Radigund's Abbey

A farmhouse now stands among the ruins of this ancient abbey at the top
of the Alkham Valley. A footpath runs close by, so you can have a look at
what's left of it. The abbey was founded in 1191 and formerly occupied
by a Premonstratensian monastic community (from Premontre near Laon
in France). Initially it became quite wealthy but later slipped into decline.
Archaeological excavations have revealed the outlines of the main complex,
including the refectory and the cellarer's domain. The most intact section is
the gatehouse, which you can see well from the path.

Reach for the Skies

Several miles further along the coast and perched on the white cliffs of
Capel-le-Ferne near Folkestone, is a striking modern memorial to the aircrew
who fought in the Battle of Britain. A statue of a pilot in flying gear sits on a
sandstone plinth, gazing out across the sea as if contemplating lost comrades.
There's a visitor centre here, with free parking and a café.

   Though not especially lengthy, this is a tough walk up steep gradients and
it can be very slippery after rain. Good footwear is essential and you need
to be fairly agile to negotiate some of the stiles. You tackle the strenuous
climbing and most of the stiles while you're fresh, then coast gently downhill
on the return leg. The rewards are breathtaking views over the dazzling
Alkham Valley, definitely worth a photograph in good weather.

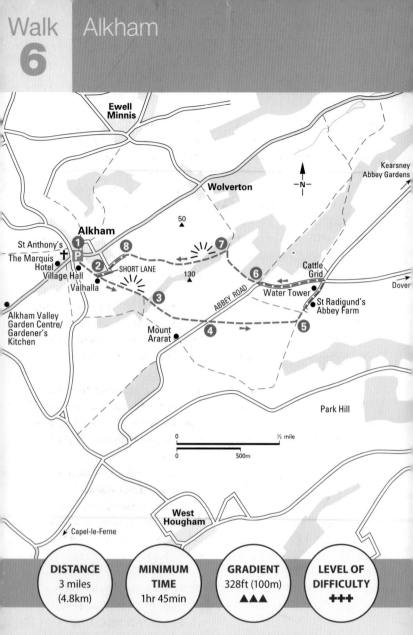

DISTANCE
3 miles
(4.8km)

MINIMUM TIME
1hr 45min

GRADIENT
328ft (100m)
▲▲▲

LEVEL OF DIFFICULTY
+++

PATHS Field and woodland paths with steep gradients, muddy after rain; some road-walking; 11 stiles (some very awkward) **LANDSCAPE** Steep chalk valley with lovely views; woods and farmland; abbey ruins **SUGGESTED MAP** OS Explorer 138 Dover, Folkestone & Hythe **START/FINISH** Grid reference: TR 256424
DOG FRIENDLINESS May run free except near stock or on roads
PARKING Village hall car park (off Hogbrook Hill opposite Marquis Hotel)
PUBLIC TOILETS None on route; nearest at Kearsney Abbey car park

WALK 6 DIRECTIONS

❶ From the car park, walk down the playing fields and turn right through a gap in the hedge at the far end, by the footbridge. Turn left along the path for a few paces until you emerge at the end of a cul-de-sac (Short Lane) by houses. Turn briefly left, cross the road and look for a fenced path running off right beside a house called Valhalla.

❷ Walk up between the houses and cross the stile into fields, then walk half left up the sloping pastureland beyond, taking stiles where necessary (there may be temporary paddock fencing here) until you reach the left corner of a patch of woodland. Skirt around the wood, bearing left where the path forks and take a stile into a belt of trees beyond (a tricky scramble; the path is steep and slippery).

❸ Follow the path through the trees, then take another stile into paddocks and continue diagonally left. The terrain is flatter now you are approaching the top of the ridge. Cross a couple of fields to reach a lane.

> 🍴 **EATING AND DRINKING**
>
> The Marquis, next to the church, is an upscale hotel-restaurant which attracts gastro-patrons from far and wide. For something a little less rarified, try the Gardener's Kitchen tea rooms at the Alkham Valley Garden Centre just along the road towards South Alkham.

❹ Cross the road and take the path opposite, bearing half left again toward barns on the crest of the hill. In 0.75 miles (1.2km) reach the corner of a field. Go through the gate towards St Radigund's Abbey Farm.

❺ Take the concrete farm track around the left of the buildings and walk past the abbey gatehouse, passing a water tower on your left and crossing a cattle grid on to a road at a junction. Turn left along Abbey Road, signed 'Capel-le-Ferne and Folkestone', and stroll gently downhill for about 500yds (457m).

❻ Bear left round a bend, then take the path on your right into the woods beyond, climbing between fields, then descending through more woodland.

❼ When you meet a crossing path, turn left and continue downhill, passing a steep bank to your right. Go through a metal gate and carry on, skirting the shoulder of the hill down to the village on a chalky path.

❽ Bear left though a gate at the end of a hedgeline and walk past some houses, soon leaving the footpath and emerging on to Short Lane, a residential road. Walk straight on, passing 'Valhalla' again on your left. You are now back on the route you followed at the start of the walk. At the end of the road, turn right along the conifer path back to the playing fields and return to the village hall car park.

RECULVER COUNTRY PARK

A breezy seaside walk around an evocative ancient monument.

A walk along this breezy strip of clifftop meadows certainly blows the cobwebs away. The route circuits a coastal country park, starting at one of North Kent's most memorable landmarks. Paths are easy to follow along well-made sections of established trails: the Saxon Shore Way, the Wantsum Walk and the more recently developed Oyster Bay Trail and Viking Coastal Trail (designed for cyclists). For much of the way, the twin towers of the remains of St Mary's Church give you your bearings.

The Two Sisters

The emblematic towers of the ruinous St Mary's Church are visible for many miles along this otherwise featureless coast. The first church on this site was a Saxon monastery founded by King Egbert, constructed from masonry pillaged from a Roman fort guarding the Wantsum Channel. The surviving Norman structure dates from about 1200. Originally each of the towers had a spire but these were destroyed in a storm. Over the centuries the Wantsum Channel silted, the coastline eroded and Reculver's population declined. Most villagers moved inland to Hillborough, where another church was built. By the early 19th century, St Mary's Church seemed to have outlived its purpose, but Trinity House (the lighthouse authority) intervened to save the west front as an important navigational seamark.

The Reculver Centre

The visitor centre in the car park has displays on many aspects of Reculver's fascinating history, wildlife and geology. The Reculver Country Park is an internationally important site for birds; sand martins make their homes in the cliffs, feeding on the insects in the clifftop meadows.

As the centre is partly funded by the Kentish Flats Wind Farm (visible offshore), there's a strong emphasis on renewable energy at this recently designed building. It is powered by solar and photovoltaic panels and a sustainable wood-burning stove fuelled by logs from Blean Woods near Canterbury. Large skylights maximise natural light levels.

Opposite: Oilseed rape near Reculver

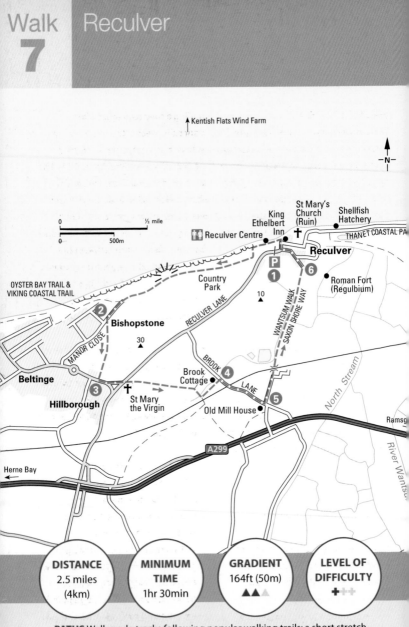

↑ Kentish Flats Wind Farm

OYSTER BAY TRAIL & VIKING COASTAL TRAIL

DISTANCE	MINIMUM TIME	GRADIENT	LEVEL OF DIFFICULTY
2.5 miles (4km)	1hr 30min	164ft (50m) ▲▲▲	✚✚✚

PATHS Well-made tracks following popular walking trails; a short stretch of quiet village street; no stiles **LANDSCAPE** Cliff tops, fields, a majestic ruin, and an offshore wind farm; interesting wildlife and geology; open views
SUGGESTED MAP OS Explorer 150 Canterbury & the Isle of Thanet
START/FINISH Grid reference: TR 226693 **DOG FRIENDLINESS** An excellent place to let dogs run free (mind they don't chase sticks or balls over the cliffs)
PARKING At Reculver car park (pay-and-display) **PUBLIC TOILETS** At the Reculver Centre **NOTE** Keep clear of the unstable cliff edges

WALK 7 DIRECTIONS

❶ From the visitor centre, follow the grassy clifftop path up the hill towards Herne Bay, keeping the sea on your right. It's a steady climb but easy going on a well-made track reinforced with plastic matting. (Note: This is part of the Viking Coastal Trail; cyclists may be coming downhill at speed.)

❷ As you approach the buildings of Bishopstone, pass through a barrier on to a tarmac path, bearing left and following Oyster Bay Trail signs past some information boards, a parking space and picnic tables on your right. When you reach Manor Close, take the footpath to your left (CH54) through a kissing gate. Head half right across the field following a track over a ditch. Continue over the next field towards modern housing ahead and a small chapel half left.

❸ Bear left near the end of the field to a corner gap in the hedge and go out to Reculver Lane. You are now in the village of Hillborough. Turn left past a thatched cottage,

---

joining a road converging from your right. Keep left past a primary school and a war memorial by the Church of St Mary the Virgin. Turn right through the church car park and take the gap in a railed fence down three steps, then follow the track ahead gently downhill, crossing a footbridge between fields. At the edge of the second field take a gap through the trees over another footbridge (several steps either side) by a railway line.

❹ Turn left via a small gate and follow the path left past Brook Cottage, turning right on to Brook Lane through a gate. Cross the railway line via the bridge and climb to the Old Mill House after 300yds (274m).

❺ Turn left on to a footpath (CH52 – part of the Saxon Shore Way), and walk along a concrete drive, ducking through a vehicle barrier and going under the railway again via a tunnel. Continue, following waymarkers half right over a farm track and stream. Take the gap beside a gate and follow the field-edge path. St Mary's towers lie directly ahead of you. Pass reedy drainage ditches and cross another stream.

❻ After about 0.75 miles (1.2km), bear left by a gate through a caravan site, heading out to Reculver Lane. Turn right and return to the car park past the King Ethelbert Inn.

> 🍴 **EATING AND DRINKING**
>
> Beside the car park at Reculver is the King Ethelbert Inn, a cream-and-green building with mellow tiles. It's a free house with a beer garden and children's playground, popular with walkers and cyclists. There's no café at the Reculver Centre but you can get a hot drink there, or some local apple juice.

MARCHING THROUGH BARHAM

A walk around one of England's most historic areas.

This walk introduces you to a forgotten corner of Kent. Barham's a pleasant village but not so picturesque that it makes it on to the standard tourist itinerary; most people have never even heard of it. Yet Barham (pronounced Bar-rum) has witnessed more historic events than many major towns and cities – and they've all had a distinctly military flavour.

A Pageant of History

The village dates from Saxon times and sits snugly by Barham Downs. The Roman legions were here first in 54 BC, camping on the Downs. The Britons fought hard to repel them but stood no chance against Caesar's mighty army. Contemporary accounts claim that every single Briton was slain.

During the Norman Conquest of 1066, William the Conqueror met the people of Kent on the Downs, to hear them swear allegiance to him. He took a few hostages at the same time, just to encourage them to keep their word. Years later King John (1167–1216) camped on Barham Downs with 50,000 men as he prepared to go to war with France and it was here, too, that Simon de Montfort gathered a huge army during the Barons' War. This began in 1264, after several powerful barons disagreed with the policies of Henry III. Led by Simon de Montfort they took up arms and captured Henry. De Montfort, a French nobleman, then took over control of England, which he ruled until he was killed in 1265.

After that Barham was a peaceful place until the outbreak of civil war, when Royalist forces assembled here in 1642 before attacking Dover Castle. And then, during the Napoleonic Wars, in the early 19th century, the army camped on the Downs before heading off to France. The soldiers seem to have made the most of the opportunites to meet the local women, because the church witnessed plenty of their weddings and baptisms.

Barham continued to act as a military magnet in the 20th century. During the First World War the fields were filled with soldiers waiting to go overseas. And in the Second World War a German aircraft crashed on to the railway line. The crew were captured by the local Home Guard.

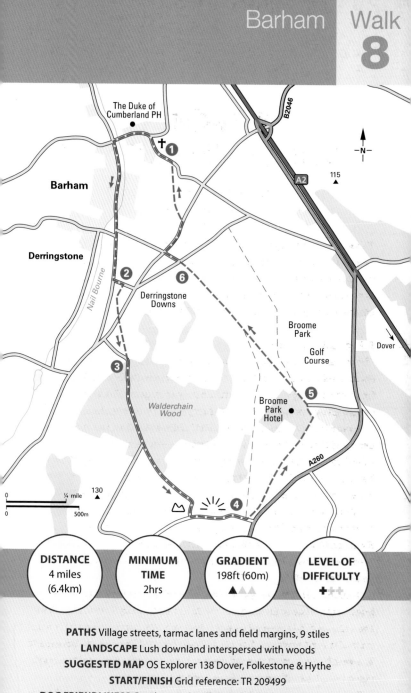

DISTANCE	MINIMUM TIME	GRADIENT	LEVEL OF DIFFICULTY
4 miles (6.4km)	2hrs	198ft (60m) ▲▲▲	✚✚✚

PATHS Village streets, tarmac lanes and field margins, 9 stiles

LANDSCAPE Lush downland interspersed with woods

SUGGESTED MAP OS Explorer 138 Dover, Folkestone & Hythe

START/FINISH Grid reference: TR 209499

DOG FRIENDLINESS Good, several stretches to run free but keep on lead when near livestock and on golf course **PARKING** By Barham church

PUBLIC TOILETS None on route

WALK 8 DIRECTIONS

❶ From the 13th-century church, with its distinctive green copper spire, walk down through the village, passing The Duke of Cumberland pub, to reach the green. Turn left along Valley Road and continue up Derringstone Hill, then turn left up Mill Lane.

❷ Take the footpath on the right beside a house, bear left, then right through an area of scrub to reach a road. Cross the stile opposite and go diagonally across the field towards the wood to join another road.

❸ Follow the road through the woods. It's very easy walking here, and although it's tarmacked you don't usually meet much traffic. Keep left at a fork by Woodcote House and soon go steeply downhill. At the bottom go left, signed 'Denton'. The lane now opens out on the right, giving pleasant views over pasture. Just before the main road there are two footpaths leading off to the left; take the one that forks right.

❹ Go through trees to a gate and keep ahead through pasture towards Broome Park Hotel. Beyond two kissing gates, follow the tarmac path between lodges, soon to bear left along the hotel drive. Go through the car park, turn left and walk in front of the house. Now a hotel and golf club, the house was originally built in the 17th century by Inigo Jones for Sir Basil Dixwell, the man who signed the

(unfulfilled) death warrant of Charles Edward Stuart (1720–88), popularly known as Bonnie Prince Charlie. In the early 20th century it became the home of Lord Kitchener of Khartoum (1850–1916), the celebrated General who gained notoriety in the First World War. He featured on the famous poster 'Your Country Needs You'.

❺ Walk up the track to the first tee, keep ahead across the fairway (look out for golf balls) and walk up to the marker post to the right of trees. Cross the next fairway ahead and go over the stile into the field. Continue along the left-hand edge, walking in the direction of Barham church. Cross another two fields and come on to the road, through a kissing gate.

> Ⓨ **EATING AND DRINKING**
> The Duke of Cumberland pub in Barham is noted for its food and, as well as serving sandwiches and coffees, offers a good range of main dishes and real ales. The pub can get busy so you are advised to book if you want to eat.

❻ Cross over to the other side and walk along the road almost directly ahead of you. At the crossroads turn right and head up the road, crossing a stile on your left to follow a footpath which brings you up to the cemetery and the road opposite the church.

THE HEART OF BISHOPSBOURNE

Discover the country home of author Joseph Conrad and a peculiar coincidence involving James Bond.

Get your boots on, synchronise your watches and pack your GPS – you probably won't need them but this walk is filled with reminders of a couple of all-action heroes; a swashbuckling sailor and a fictional spy.

A Seafaring Smuggler

Polish writer Joseph Conrad (1857–1924) came to Bishopsbourne in 1919. He was the author of many novels but could hardly have invented a more entertaining story than that of his own life. Born Jósef Teodor Konrad Nalecz Korzeniowski in 1857 in Berdichev, Poland (now in the Ukraine), Conrad lost both his parents at an early age. He left Poland as soon as he could and went to Marseilles to join the French merchant navy. Conrad travelled widely and was involved with smuggling and running guns to supporters of Don Carlos VII, who was trying to claim the Spanish throne.

Shortly before he was 21 Conrad took a job on a British ship. He learned English, passed his captain's exams and in 1884 became a naturalised British subject. He travelled to remote places, such as Borneo, Singapore and Australia. He also went up river in the Belgian Congo, a part of Africa known as the 'white man's graveyard'. This inspired his novel *Heart of Darkness* but also seriously undermined his health.

Eventually Conrad gave up his rather wild seafaring ways and settled down quietly in Kent. He took to writing and spent the last five years of his life at Bishopsbourne, living at Oswalds, a house by the church.

One of Conrad's novels was entitled *The Secret Agent* (1907) and he probably would have made a great James Bond. By coincidence, one of the James Bond books, *You Only Live Twice* (1964) was written at the Duck pub at nearby Pett Bottom. Ian Fleming, who wrote the books, lived in Kent, when he wasn't living in Jamaica, and frequently took his inspiration from the area. In fact James Bond's code name was taken from the number 007 bus that ran by Fleming's home near Dover. Whether the Duck ever served martinis – shaken, not stirred – but if he'd been around Joseph Conrad would no doubt have tried one.

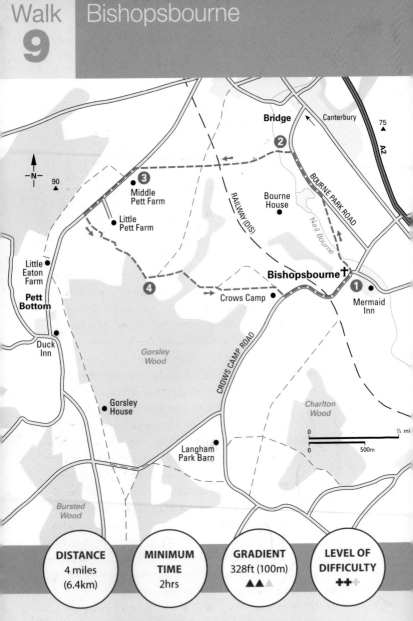

BOURNE PARK ROAD

—N—

90 ▲

❸
Middle Pett Farm

● Little Pett Farm

Bourne House ●

RAILWAY (D/S)

Nail Bourne

❷

Little Eaton Farm ●

Pett Bottom

❹

Crows Camp ●

Bishopsbourne †

❶

Mermaid Inn

● Duck Inn

Gorsley Wood

CROWS CAMP ROAD

● Gorsley House

Charlton Wood

0 .... ½ mi
0 .... 500m

● Langham Park Barn

Bursted Wood

DISTANCE	MINIMUM TIME	GRADIENT	LEVEL OF DIFFICULTY
4 miles (6.4km)	2hrs	328ft (100m) ▲▲▲	++ +

PATHS Narrow lanes, field and woodland paths
LANDSCAPE Country house parkland, agricultural fields and orchards
SUGGESTED MAPS OS Explorer 150 Canterbury & the Isle of Thanet,
Explorer 138 Dover **START/FINISH** Grid reference: TR 187526
DOG FRIENDLINESS On lead through grazed areas and if notices indicate
PARKING Bishopsbourne, by the church or near Mermaid Inn
PUBLIC TOILETS None on route

WALK 9 DIRECTIONS

❶ From the church, walk through the graveyard following the Elham Valley Way. Have a look for the grave of the Revd Joseph Bancroft Reade. A rector of the church and one of only a handful of religious men who felt that Darwin's theory of evolution did not go against the teachings of the Bible. Go through a gate, then at a waymarker bear right across pasture to cross a bridge over the Nail Bourne. Pass through another gate and continue through parkland of Bourne House, passing the lake on your left, to reach a gate and turn left into Bourne Park Road. Stroll past the gates of Bourne House and continue until you reach two cottages on the right.

🍴 EATING AND DRINKING

The Mermaid Inn at Bishopsbourne serves excellent lunches. You can also divert from Point ❸ to visit the Duck Inn at Pett Bottom, which serves good food. The nearby village of Bridge has several pubs and a good bakery.

---

❷ Turn left down the lane and cross the stream again. Follow the lane until it peters out near a farm and hop gardens, then continue ahead between the hedges. There's a gentle climb now, across a bridge and uphill along the edge of a field. Cross a stile at the right-hand corner, then descend into the valley walking diagonally over the fields towards the distant high hedge.

---

❷ IN THE AREA

Bishopsbourne church dates back to the 13th century. It has medieval floor tiles, stained glass and wall paintings. Take a look at the west window by the Arts and Crafts artists Edward Burne-Jones and William Morris.

Go through the hedge, cross straight over the field towards the oast house, bearing right in the next field to reach the lane. Turn left and walk along the road to Middle Pett Farm.

❸ Continue ahead, pass Little Pett Farm and then turn left to head up the footpath. Cross a stile at the top left-hand corner of a field and follow the left-hand margin of the next field. Cross a stile on the left, then walk left around the next field and continue uphill through the next field towards the corner of the woodland. Follow the left-hand side of the wood and, after about 400yds (366m), turn sharp left, away from the wood and cross the field to the marker post by the holly hedge.

❹ Ignore the stile and fork right across the field, following the track into woodland. Emerge into open fields and soon go sharp left. Fork right at the first telegraph pole and walk across a large field heading towards the chimneys of Crows Camp ahead. Pass to the left of the garden hedge, turn left at the road and walk back into Bishopsbourne.

IN SEARCH OF ELHAM'S SECRET STREAM

A varied walk through open countryside that takes
you over an elusive stream and up to an ancient church.

Although you'll cross the course of the Nail Bourne on both the outward and
return legs of this walk, the chances are that you won't be aware of it – for
this is Kent's most elusive stream and it only flows in the wettest winters. The
waters (bourne is an old local word for stream) used to be known as the Woe
Waters, for their flow was once believed to herald death or disaster.

Battle of the Gods

The Nail Bourne has strong associations with the conversion of Kent to
Christianity. Although some Britons became Christians during the Roman
occupation (AD 43–406), the country gradually returned to paganism when
the Romans left. When St Augustine came to this part of England in AD 597
to convert the Anglo-Saxons to Christianity, the county had experienced an
extended period of drought. Crops had failed, animals had died and the local
people began to feel that their interest in this new religion had offended their
pagan gods. The Christian priests, sensing trouble, hastily began to pray for
rain. Legend has it that, on the spot where St Augustine knelt to pray, a spring
miraculously appeared and flowed through what is now the Elham Valley.
Furious at this display of Christian power, the pagan gods were said to have
dried the stream, which God, just as promptly, made flow again.

In fact, the Nail Bourne is an example of a winterbourne – a seasonal stream
that is a distinctive feature of chalklands. They occur because chalk is porous
and rain quickly seeps down through it and disappears from view. However,
if there is a thick layer of clay further down, a spring develops. This spring will
only turn into a stream if it is extremely wet – so winterbournes appear and
disappear as if by magic.

An Ancient Church

The Church of St Mary the Virgin in Elham is well worth a look. It dates
back to 1180 and has some unusual 19th-century stained glass, in which
contemporary figures are portrayed as characters from the Bible. Look closely
and you'll see Thomas Carlyle, William Gladstone and Benjamin Disraeli.

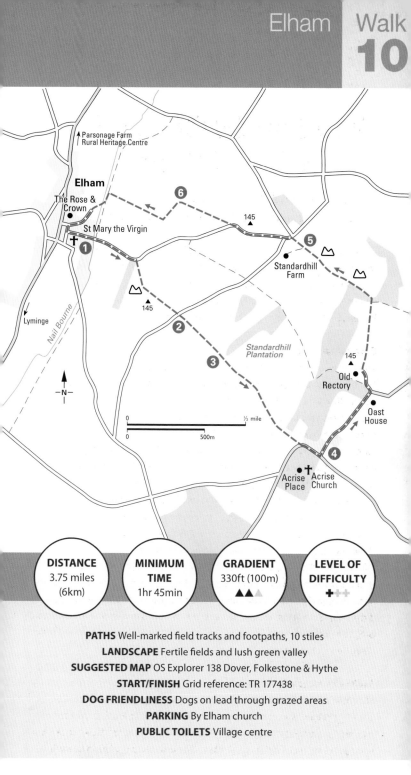

WALK 10 DIRECTIONS

1 From the church walk down Duck Street, then head uphill to a footpath on the right. Cross the stile and continue uphill, then cross another stile at the top of the field. Walk straight ahead and cross two more stiles to the road.

2 Cross here and follow the footpath ahead, through a gate, then along the field-edge – if it's just been ploughed you'll see plenty of flints exposed. The path goes downhill to a stile and then ahead along the field past a pylon.

3 Go past a small wood, through a gate and continue straight across the large field ahead. Drop down to another stile into an army training area, then walk up the edge of a wood. At the corner of the trees, walk straight up the field to a stile and the road. Walk ahead to the crossroads (you can make a detour right through the trees to Acrise church).

4 Otherwise turn left and continue until you pass an old oast house. Turn left just after this, then take the right-hand path to the Old Rectory, signed 'Private Road'. Go over a stile immediately in front of the house, then cross a meadow. After a further stile your route leads diagonally over a field. After a gate, turn left and walk along a field-edge. After another gate the path goes steeply downhill to the

> **🍴 EATING AND DRINKING**
>
> The Rose and Crown is a friendly pub serving Shepherd Neame ales and a good range of pub food, from thick-cut sandwiches and decent ploughman's lunches to home-made burgers and daily specials.

valley bottom, then rises again, just as steeply, to join a concrete track up to the farm. Where the track bears left, you go right and through a gate and up to the farm buildings. Go through a gate and turn left when you reach the road.

5 At the house turn right and go along the road under a line of pylons. Just after a copse the lane bears left. Take the footpath ahead down the edge of a field. Bear diagonally left across another field following the clearly marked path and at the bottom left-hand corner go over a stile with a rather long drop.

6 Head along the edge of the field, keeping the fence on your right. Follow the fence and at the corner follow it downhill and over another stile. Head straight across the next field and bear left along the field-edge. You'll come to a gate which takes you over a stone bridge. Walk diagonally across the field in the direction of the church. One more gate brings you up to a lane and back to the church.

A CANTERBURY TRAIL

Canterbury's streets have attracted
pilgrims for centuries.

As you walk through the streets of Canterbury, you can't help but be aware
that you are following in the footsteps of millions of pilgrims. They have been
drawn to Canterbury cathedral every year since 1170, when Thomas Becket
was murdered at the cathedral and have included some notable historic
figures. Yet, out of all these people, the most famous pilgrims of all are
fictional – they are the characters created by Geoffrey Chaucer (c1345–1400)
in his epic poem *The Canterbury Tales* (1387).

Roving Ambassador

Chaucer is acknowledged as the father of English literature but writing
wasn't his main occupation, it was just a hobby. Chaucer was born while
the Hundred Years War was raging between England and France and, after
several years working in the Royal household, he joined the army. He was
taken prisoner in France but was released after the English paid a ransom for
him. Chaucer then became a sort of roving ambassador travelling throughout
Europe on various high level diplomatic missions. He could read French, Latin
and Italian and when he travelled he took the opportunity to study foreign
literature, which he put to good use in his own works. Back in England, he
took on various official posts, including customs controller of furs, skins and
hides, and knight of the shire for Kent. He also found time to write several
long poems and translate many works of prose.

He wrote *The Canterbury Tales* around 1387 and created a cast of lively,
believable characters that tell us a great deal about life in the 14th century.
There's the earthy Wife of Bath, who's already had five husbands and seems
to have set out on this pilgrimage to catch her sixth; the too worldly Prioress,
who puts on affected table manners and speaks French – unfortunately
more like Del Boy Trotter than anything else; and then there's the corrupt
Friar, who's not at all bothered about those in need, but who sells absolution
to anyone who can afford it. The poem, written in Middle English, became
the first printed work of English literature and is known all over the world.
Chaucer is buried in Westminster Abbey.

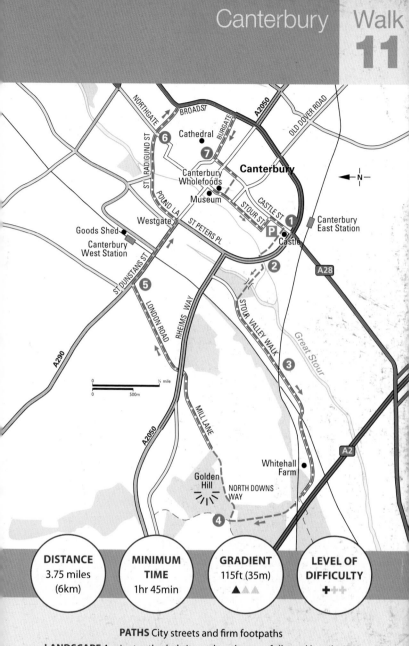

DISTANCE	MINIMUM TIME	GRADIENT	LEVEL OF DIFFICULTY
3.75 miles (6km)	1hr 45min	115ft (35m) ▲▲▲	+++

PATHS City streets and firm footpaths
LANDSCAPE Ancient cathedral city and tracks once followed by pilgrims
SUGGESTED MAP OS Explorer 150 Canterbury & the Isle of Thanet
START/FINISH Grid reference: TR 146574
DOG FRIENDLINESS Keep on lead in city but can mostly run free on footpaths
PARKING Castle Street or one of several car parks in Canterbury
PUBLIC TOILETS Castle Row, off Burgate and off High Street

Opposite: Canterbury Cathedral

WALK 11 DIRECTIONS

❶ Go right from Castle Street car park then right again down Gas Street to pass the castle. At the end turn left on Centenary Walk. Where this finishes go right and walk beside the road. Cross a bridge, turn left, go under another bridge and along the river to the other side of the road.

❷ Cross some grassland then a bridge and through a play area. Walk across the car park and turn left up the road to join the Stour Valley Walk.

❸ Go under a bridge and continue to a level crossing. Cross the railway, then stroll up past Whitehall Farm. Go under the bridge, through a gate and over a stream. The path bends round and the main road is on your left. At a junction turn right along the North Downs Way.

❹ Go over a bridge and up a lane. To your left is Golden Hill – from which pilgrims traditionally had their first view of the city. When you come to a track, turn left and follow it round. Go right along Mill Lane to the main road. Take the underpass to cross Rheims Way, walk down London Road, then turn right into St Dunstans Street.

❺ Walk into Canterbury to the Westgate, turn left along Pound Lane and into St Radigund Street.

❻ Continue into Northgate, go left then right down Broad Street. You're now walking around the city walls. Turn right along Burgate, past a tiny 16th-century building called the Pilgrim's Shop. Soon come to a pedestrianised area that brings you out at the Butter Market and war memorial. On your right is the entrance to the cathedral.

❼ Turn left, cross The Parade into St Margaret's Street and turn right down Beer Cart Lane. Turn left into Stour Street and on the right is the museum and almost opposite, down Jewry Lane, is Canterbury Wholefoods where you can finish your walk. To return to Castle Street, retrace your steps along Stour Street, turn left on Rosemary Lane then right back to the car park.

> ### ⍟ EATING AND DRINKING
> Canterbury Wholefoods on Jewry Lane has a café upstairs, with organic cakes and snacks. The Goods Shed at Canterbury's West Station is a daily farmers' market with an all-day eatery serving meals made from market produce.

> ### ⚘ ON THE WALK
> Canterbury Cathedral was the first cathedral built in England. It was founded in AD 597 by St Augustine. The present structure dates back to 1071 and is a spectacular example of ecclesiastical architecture.

ON SAFARI
NEAR HYTHE

Exotic animals and ancient buildings
on a walk near the Royal Military Canal.

Less than a 1,000 years ago, Hythe's High Street was a bustling Cinque Port quayside. Not far from the walk route on the B2067 stands a war memorial known as the Shepway Cross erected in 1923 to honour the dead of the First World War. It is believed to stand on the old meeting place of the Court of Shepway, over which the Lord Warden of the Cinque Ports presided during the Middle Ages.

This walk passes through the wildlife park at Port Lympne, where you'll almost certainly meet a few of its inhabitants, and some countryside with a highly unusual geology and a history, too. The first section follows the Royal Military Canal west of Hythe, scarcely wavering above sea level. You then ascend a sharp incline to the top of an inland cliff, giving grandstand views over Romney Marsh to the sea. The manorial village of Lympne is a medieval time warp and there are glimpses of older buildings on the slopes below.

The Royal Military Canal

This grand project formed part of the defences against a possible Napoleonic invasion in the early 19th century. Romney Marsh seemed an obvious place for troops to land, so the 28-mile (45km) canal was laboriously constructed by hand between 1804 and 1809. The earth dug out of the trench was piled up alongside as a rampart from which troops could fire at invading forces but the steep terrain immediately behind the canal created an even more formidable natural barrier. Now fully restored, it has taken on a new lease of life as a leisure and wildlife site. It also controls the drainage of Romney Marsh.

Port Lympne

The late John Aspinall's animal park occupies a 600-acre (243ha) site in the grounds of a 1920s mansion. It promises a great family day out and claims a serious conservation role in protecting and breeding endangered animals, where possible returning them to the wild. The philosophy behind its 'African Experience' is to allow species to roam freely as they would in their native habitats. Prize exhibits include herds of black rhino and Przewalski horses.

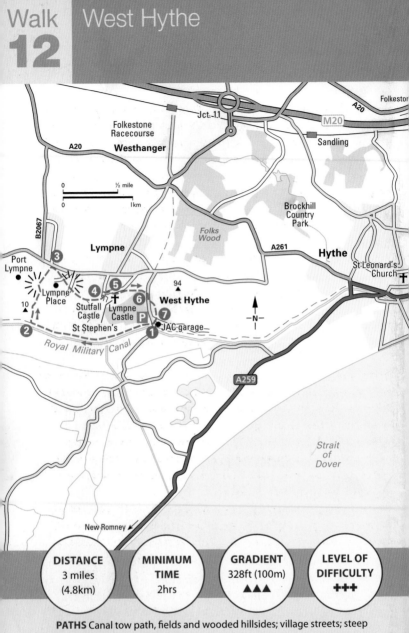

DISTANCE
3 miles
(4.8km)

MINIMUM
TIME
2hrs

GRADIENT
328ft (100m)
▲▲▲

LEVEL OF
DIFFICULTY
+++

PATHS Canal tow path, fields and wooded hillsides; village streets; steep gradients; 3 stiles **LANDSCAPE** Scenic waterfront and wooded cliff, with some unexpected wildlife **SUGGESTED MAP** OS Explorer Dover, Folkestone & Hythe **START/FINISH** Grid reference: TR 124342

DOG FRIENDLINESS Should be kept under control in orchards, near stock or on roads **PARKING** West Hythe car park (by the canal bridge) **PUBLIC TOILETS** None on route; nearest in Hythe, near The Green on the corner of Chapel Street, or at the library/museum

WALK 12 DIRECTIONS

1 From the car park at West Hythe, take the tow path westwards for just over a mile (1.6km). On the first section of the walk, two paths run parallel along the canal, one a bridleway, the other a raised bank for walkers (the latter is dryer and smoother, with better views of the waterfront). Pass a footbridge on your left after about 800yds (732m), and shortly afterwards, look out for the crumbling masonry of an old Roman fort to your right. Ignore a footpath to the right at this point and carry on along the tow path.

2 After a mile (1.6km) or so, look out for strange creatures in the grounds of Port Lympne, right. Watch carefully for a footpath signed to your right, over a wooden footbridge. Start a steady climb uphill. The track weaves a bit but is easy to follow and strongly fenced to either side, especially at the elephant enclosure towards the top. At one point there is a crossing point with gates where Port Lympne staff can take vehicles or animals from one side to the other. The path now gets steeper.

🍴 EATING AND DRINKING

Your only option near the walk route is a roadside pub called The County Members at Lympne, fine for keeping urgent pangs of hunger or thirst at bay. Otherwise, your best bet is to head for Hythe, where you'll find a wider choice of eating places around the High Street.

---

3 Eventually the path levels and you will reach a road. Just before this, take the footpath signed to your right and walk through woodland past post-and-wire fencing. Cross the drive to Lympne Place and carry on over another lane. Continue ahead, ignoring the steep path adjoining on your right.

4 The path now skirts the edge of more woods. Follow it bearing left through offset rails towards the houses of Lympne. Go out to the road and turn right passing Lympne Castle. Walk through St Stephen's churchyard.

5 Take the gate at the far side, turning right on the lane and right again over a footpath stile in a few paces. Head downhill on a steep uneven track, crossing another stile at the edge of the trees. Now go half left down sloping pasture to the road below.

6 Take another stile at the field-edge, turn right on the road, Lympne Hill, and walk downhill. At a house called Long Barrow on your left, a footpath leads past a 1930s art deco-style house (it's hard to spot). Keep left here and follow the path down a long narrow field with a brook on your left. Take another stile at the bottom and emerge on the road at a junction by a garage, JAC Motor Enterprises.

7 Bear right down the main road for a few paces until you reach the car park just before the bridge.

A HISTORIC ROUTE MARCH FROM CHARTHAM HATCH

Take to the trails through woods and orchards
near an ancient battleground.

Several long distance trails run through Chartham and its neighbour Chartham Hatch. This walk covers a section of the North Downs Way (towards the final stage of the old pilgrim route to Canterbury) and the Stour Valley Walk following the river past flooded gravel pits. On the way you pass lots of orchards (ancient and modern) and the site of the momentous Battle of Bigbury – Caesar's first serious attack on Britain after the conquest of Gaul.

No Man's Orchard

This walk takes you through a traditional apple orchard. Many of Kent's old fruit trees have long since been replaced with other crops but this 10-acre (4ha) site is a rare survival of an orchard planted soon after the Second World War. It is now designated as a Site of Nature Conservation Interest and managed by local authorities with public access. Display boards explain the background and history of this recently restored community orchard, which got its name because the parish boundary runs across the middle, splitting the land between its former owners, so it didn't belong to any single person.

These huge, gnarled apple trees belong to many old-fashioned varieties and are still productive, despite their great age. Over 150 trees are Bramleys but other varieties act as pollinators (James Grieve, Worcester, Howgate Wonder). No toxic sprays are used on the trees, so the fruit is organic and the site supports lots of wildlife. No Man's Orchard is predictably popular when the fruit ripens but also lovely in late spring when the blossom is out.

The Battle of Bigbury

Deep in the woods of Bigbury lie the remains of an Iron Age camp, believed to be the site where Julius Caesar fought the Celtic Cantium tribe soon after invading Britain in AD 54. There isn't much to see there now, though the surrounding woods are steadily being cleared to give a better view of the camp from the North Downs Way. But it was certainly a significant battle. If the ancient Britons had managed to repel the Romans at this point, our history might have been altogether different.

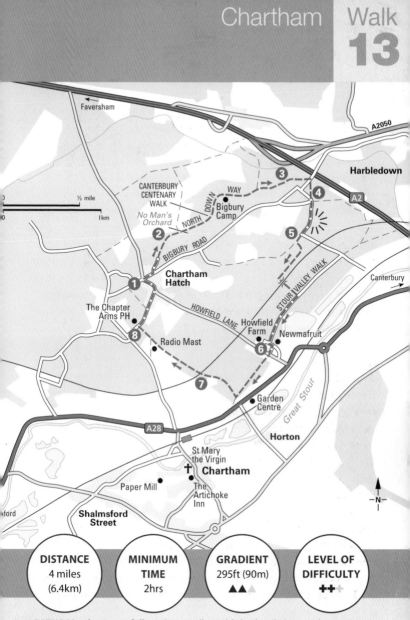

DISTANCE	MINIMUM TIME	GRADIENT	LEVEL OF DIFFICULTY
4 miles (6.4km)	2hrs	295ft (90m) ▲▲▲	✚✚✚

PATHS Mostly easy to follow along well-established trails (one tricky section through orchards); steepish gradients; 8 stiles **LANDSCAPE** Woodland, fields and orchards **SUGGESTED MAP** OS Explorer 150 Canterbury & the Isle of Thanet **START/FINISH** Grid reference: TR 105567 **DOG FRIENDLINESS** Keep under control in orchards, near stock or on roads **PARKING** Street parking on Howfield Lane **PUBLIC TOILETS** Station Road, Chartham village **NOTE** Some of the orchard paths are tricky. Look carefully for waymarked posts. If you lose your bearings, head to the edge of the orchard and walk round it until you rejoin the path

WALK 13 DIRECTIONS

❶ From the bus shelter on Howfield Lane, walk right down Bigbury Road, signed 'Pilgrims Way' towards Harbledown. In about 100yds (91m), bear left between houses on a path marked 'North Downs Way'. Head right past a recreation field and take a path beside a tall conifer hedge and a chainlink fence.

❷ Follow the path downhill through woodland, soon entering No Man's Orchard. Walk up its left-hand edge, bearing left at the end through a kissing gate on to a sandy path. Follow the well-made trail through the woods for about a mile (1.6km), past ferns and coppiced chestnut. To your right, signs indicate Bigbury Camp.

❸ At the edge of the woods, you will see (and hear) traffic on the nearby A2. Turn right and carry on until you reach a lane. Cross over and take the path through a kissing gate to your right. Keeping a hedge on your left, walk through fields over a couple of stiles. When you reach the metalled road at a junction in about 200yds (183m), take the left-hand fork and walk downhill past orchards. To your left you will see Canterbury in the distance.

❹ At a sharp left-hand bend, leave the lane and take the footpath ahead, signed 'Centenary Walk', past the security gates of Kenlicote House. After about 50 paces, take the path to your left into a field (collapsed stile here) and bear right through orchards down to the railway line. Keep this on your left and walk along it until you reach a tunnel on your left leading under the line.

❺ Go through the tunnel and walk up to a metalled byway, marked 'Stour Valley Walk'. Turn right here, passing old gravel working lakes in the Stour Valley below you. Keep going past Newmafruit, a fruit-growing business.

❻ Follow the path past storage sheds, bearing right briefly on to Howfield Lane. Cross and turn left at a footpath sign between houses. Go straight on through orchards. When you pass a green building marked 'Garden Centre' visible to your left on the nearby road (A28), turn right on the waymarked track through the orchard (a steep climb) into a patch of woodland.

❼ Look for a stile when you reach the railway line and climb some steps. Cross the line (take great care – there's no footbridge here). Turn left along a chainlink fence to another stile, then right up the edge of the wood, heading towards a radio mast ahead. Keeping the trees to your right and the mast on your left, continue through more orchards, then up a drive on to a road.

❽ Turn right past the Chapter Arms pub, emerging via New Town Street on to Howfield Lane. Turn left to the start.

A SPOOKY SAUNTER ROUND DUNGENESS

Lighthouses and a light railway
in a weird shingle desert.

The huge shingle spit at the edge of Romney Marsh may not look terribly inviting at first sight, its skyline littered with fishermen's shacks and two massive nuclear reactors. Yet these windswept drifts of pebbles are both extraordinary and curiously alluring. You can enjoy its strange scenery simply as one of Britain's wildest places (Dungeness is classified as the UK's only desert – the climate is very dry). But there's no shortage of things to see and do – a great variety of wildlife, a bizarre assortment of buildings and a magical little railway.

Prominent Landmarks

One thing you are unlikely to do is lose your bearings. Two lighthouses and that rather conspicuous power station make signposts redundant. Which is just as well – many of the footpaths here are unsigned and barely visible. Do as the locals do, and find your own way around.

The Romney, Hythe & Dymchurch Railway

One of the best things to do around Dungeness is to take a ride on one of the world's smallest public railways, which terminates by the old lighthouse. It's a thoroughly enjoyable trip for children of all ages and always very popular. The 13.5 miles (22km) line carries over 100,000 passengers a year down the coast of Romney Marsh, a seven-stop journey from its northerly terminus at Hythe.

Dungeness has achieved something like cult status in recent years, partly due to the arrival of a group of artists who have settled here to paint or write. Best-known of these was the film-director and gay activist Derek Jarman, who spent his last years at Prospect Cottage. In these desolate, salt-sprayed surroundings, he managed to create a charming shingle garden studded with driftwood and *objets trouvés* from the beach. The little fisherman's house of tarred timber with its bright yellow paintwork is easily spotted on the beach road near the lifeboat station. It isn't open to the public but you can have a look at the garden from outside.

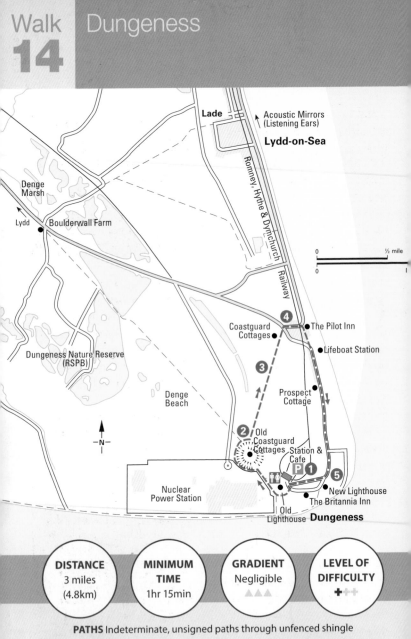

Lade

Acoustic Mirrors (Listening Ears)

Lydd-on-Sea

Denge Marsh

Lydd · Boulderwall Farm

Romney, Hythe & Dymchurch Railway

½ mile

4 Coastguard Cottages

The Pilot Inn

Lifeboat Station

3

Dungeness Nature Reserve (RSPB)

Prospect Cottage

Denge Beach

2 Old Coastguard Cottages

—N—

Station & Cafe

1 P

5

Nuclear Power Station

New Lighthouse
The Britannia Inn

Old Lighthouse · **Dungeness**

DISTANCE	MINIMUM TIME	GRADIENT	LEVEL OF DIFFICULTY
3 miles (4.8km)	1hr 15min	Negligible ▲▲▲	+++

PATHS Indeterminate, unsigned paths through unfenced shingle and scrubland; some road walking; no stiles **LANDSCAPE** Vegetated shingle beach **SUGGESTED MAP** OS Explorer 125 Romney Marsh, Rye & Winchelsea **START/FINISH** Grid reference: TR 089169 **DOG FRIENDLINESS** May run free except on road; dogs are not allowed on the RSPB nature trails inland **PARKING** By the old lighthouse (free) **PUBLIC TOILETS** At the Romney, Hythe & Dymchurch Railway (RHDR) station **NOTE** The power station site is strictly off-limits and security is high. Rights of way run close to the plant on three sides

WALK 14 DIRECTIONS

1 From the car park, walk around the base of the old lighthouse and pick up the path leading along the perimeter of the power station. Head towards the grey-roofed Old Coastguard Cottages, which are surrounded by what looks like a circular earthwork or rampart near by. The right of way leads around the base of this mound to the left of the houses; don't go through the cottage gardens, which are private.

2 As you emerge on the far side of the 'earthwork', head half right across the shingle, where a faint causeway track leads through a gap in a line of posts ahead (a dismantled railway). Continue towards a gap into bushes ahead.

3 Follow the slightly raised path ahead through the undergrowth and emerge on the shingle banks again. To your right is a scattering of shoreline shacks; make for a cluster of more substantial-looking buildings ahead of you.

4 When you pass the Coastguard Cottages on your left and reach a road by a telegraph pole, turn right towards the Pilot Inn, then right again along the access road leading back towards the lighthouses. You can if you wish take various boardwalk tracks across the shingle to have a closer look at the seafront. You will pass the lifeboat station on your left and Derek Jarman's brightly painted Prospect Cottage further down on your right.

5 Have a glance at the new lighthouse before returning to your starting point beyond the Britannia Inn.

ⓨ EATING AND DRINKING

There are two pubs at Dungeness: the Britannia Inn near the lighthouse and the well-known Pilot Inn on the Greatstone road. 'Fission chips', as it's ghoulishly known around here, is the obvious choice on the menu. For a simple snack, head for the Light Railway Café by the RHDR station (sandwiches, drinks, pies etc).

ⓞ IN THE AREA

In old gravel workings at Lade north of Dungeness, you may like to track down some peculiar structures like upturned coconut shells. Three acoustic mirrors, known as 'listening ears', were built in the 1920s and 30s as an early-warning system to detect hostile aircraft. You can visit them on free guided walks in summer.

ⓛ ON THE WALK

Close to the walk route, at Boulderwall Farm, is the Dungeness Nature Reserve, a 2,300-acre (932ha) site of flooded gravel pits, reed beds, willow scrub and shingle dunes full of seabirds and wildfowl. The visitor centre is free (there's a shop and an observation room with telescopes and identification charts) but there's a fee to go round the reserve (RSPB members free).

Old fishing boat on the shingle beach at Dungeness

THE HOLY MAID OF ALDINGTON

There are memories of a forgotten visionary
and a notorious gang of smugglers on this walk.

It's never been easy being a visionary – as one woman from Aldington found
to her cost. Her name was Elizabeth Barton and she was born in 1506, a time
when superstition, politics and religion were closely intertwined. When
Elizabeth was young she was taken on as a servant in the household of
Thomas Cobb, the Archbishop of Canterbury's local steward who looked after
the Archbishop's Palace that once stood here.

A Tudor Mystic Meg

In 1525 Elizabeth began to suffer from fits and would go into trances. When
she came round she would tell people about events or mention strange
images she had seen. Elizabeth began to make her 'prophecies' known and
hundreds of pilgrims were soon flocking to Aldington.

Elizabeth was credited with some minor miracles and William Warham, the
Archbishop of Canterbury, became interested in her visions. She was allotted
a cell at a convent in Canterbury and became known as the Holy Maid of
Kent. Unfortunately for her, the Church was in turmoil at the time, as Henry
VIII was planning to divorce his wife, Catherine of Aragon, and marry Anne
Boleyn. The authorities realised that Elizabeth's visions gave them the ideal
opportunity to prevent the marriage and stop England breaking away from
the Catholic Church. Elizabeth was poor and uneducated and they could see
that she would be easy to manipulate. They encouraged her to prophesise
that if the marriage to Anne went ahead, Henry would lose his kingdom.

The Archbishop of Canterbury, who had supported Elizabeth, was arrested
and his successor, Thomas Cranmer, set up a commission to investigate her
prophesies. The inquiry took months and in the end Elizabeth was forced to
confess – no doubt aided by gentle torture – that she had never had visions
at all. Along with several of the monks who had installed her at Canterbury,
she was tried for treason and in April 1534 they were all executed at Tyburn in
London. Elizabeth was aged just 28. Today, few people have heard of Kent's
unfortunate oracle and the Archbishop's Palace has crumbled away. You walk
past what remains of it at Court Lodge Farm, near the rather lonely church.

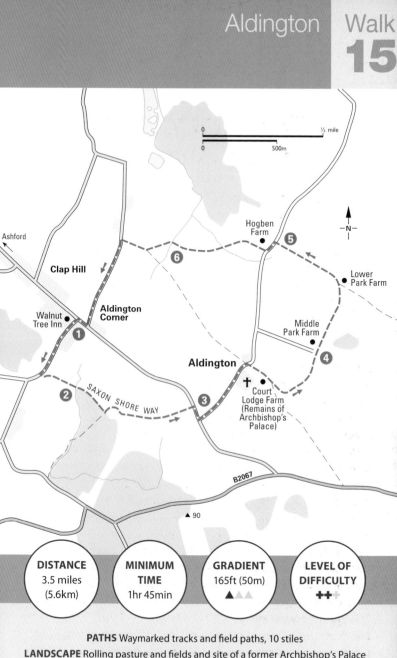

Ashford

Clap Hill

Hogben
Farm

5

6

—N—

Lower
Park Farm

Walnut
Tree Inn

**Aldington
Corner**

1

Middle
Park Farm

Aldington

4

SAXON SHORE WAY

2

3

Court
Lodge Farm
(Remains of
Archbishop's
Palace)

B2067

▲ 90

DISTANCE
3.5 miles
(5.6km)

**MINIMUM
TIME**
1hr 45min

GRADIENT
165ft (50m)
▲ ▲ ▲

**LEVEL OF
DIFFICULTY**
+ + +

PATHS Waymarked tracks and field paths, 10 stiles
LANDSCAPE Rolling pasture and fields and site of a former Archbishop's Palace
SUGGESTED MAP OS Explorer 137 Ashford
START/FINISH Grid reference: TQ 063365
DOG FRIENDLINESS Keep on lead
PARKING On street in Aldington
PUBLIC TOILETS None on route

WALK 15 DIRECTIONS

① From the Walnut Tree Inn at Aldington Corner, walk along Forge Hill. At a path on the left cross a stile to join the Saxon Shore Way. Cross the field, then a stile, turn left and follow a waymarker downhill along a field edge. Cross a stile into the woods.

② Walk through the woods, climb over a stile and, still on the Saxon Shore Way, follow the fence line, then bear left to cross a stile and a plank bridge on the right. Bear diagonally left and walk uphill through pasture between pylons to a gate. Maintain direction to reach another gate and the road.

> **🍴 EATING AND DRINKING**
>
> The Walnut Tree Inn at Aldington Corner is owned by Shepherd Neame, Britain's oldest brewer. The usual bar snacks like jacket potatoes, baguettes and sandwiches are available alongside lasagne, steak and Stilton pie and Sunday roasts.

③ Turn right then go left along the road to Aldington Church. Pass the church and take the track opposite Street Farm past cottages. This was once the site of an Archbishop's Palace but there's nothing to be seen of it today. Continue to a gate, go along the track, then follow the treeline down to a stile. Bear diagonally left across a field, then follow the field-edge to a gate at Middle Park Farm.

④ Walk through the farm and two gates, then walk along the left-hand edge of a field. Just before pylons, cross a stile on the left and continue along the field-edge, crossing a stile and plank bridge. Soon follow the grassy path left in front Lower Park Farm to join a shingle track and follow this to a gate and the road.

⑤ Turn left down the road, then turn right on to the drive of Hogben Farm. Turn immediately left through the gate by the hedge and cross the paddock to a gate. Pass in front of the house, following the marked path left to another gate. Keep ahead, cross a footbridge and bear right along a track to cross double stiles in the hedgerow on your right. Bear half-left across the field, passing under power cables to a gate in the field corner.

⑥ Cross the stile immediately on your left and bear diagonally right across the field to a gate. Follow the left-hand field-edge to a gate and turn left along the road and back into the village.

> **🌿 IN THE AREA**
>
> If you've got children with you, promise them a visit to the South of England Rare Breeds Centre at Woodchurch, a short drive from Aldington. Set in extensive grounds there are lots of traditional breeds of farm animals, including all seven of Britain's rare pigs. There are also cattle, horses, goats, poultry and rabbits.

ACROSS ROMNEY MARSHES

An atmospheric walk across moody marshlands.

The flat, windy marshlands, topped with sweeping skies, present an unusual picture in southern England. Stretching endlessly to the horizon, the marshes are laced with watery hollows and quiet footpaths, and dotted with the ruins of abandoned churches. The light here takes on an eerie clarity and even the buildings are different with small, squat churches and secretive little houses, that look as if they are trying to shrink into the landscape. Romney Marsh was originally an expanse of ever-changing salt marsh and tidal creeks, reclaimed from the sea first by the Romans and then the Saxons – the name is thought to derive from the Saxon 'Rumnea' meaning marsh water.

Historic Marsh Village

This walk takes you between two historic marsh villages, starting at Ivychurch. The inn sits next to St George's Church, built in the 1360s. It's quiet today but it hasn't always been this sleepy. During the Civil War, Cromwell's soldiers slept here and even stabled their horses in the church. In later years, when smugglers roamed the marshes, churches were often used to hide contraband such as tea and spirits. St George's was certainly used as a hiding place. At one time the vicar was unable to take Sunday service because, according to the sexton the 'pulpit be full o' baccy and vestry be full o' brandy'. In those days tea was so expensive that locals couldn't afford it, so they made their own version with local herbs. During the Second World War the church was used as a secret food store in case the country was invaded. Inside the church you can see some stone seats along one wall. These were reserved for the elderly in the days before churches had pews.

Along the way, look out for some distinctive local plants. Marsh mallow plants grow by ditches and produce soft pink flowers in July and August. The roots of the plant were once used to make sticky sweets – the forerunners of the commercial marshmallows we can buy today. Along the lanes, look for blackthorn hedges, that were planted to supply wood to pack the sea walls. So much wood was needed that it became an offence to chop blackthorn without permission. Anyone who was caught doing so had an ear cut off.

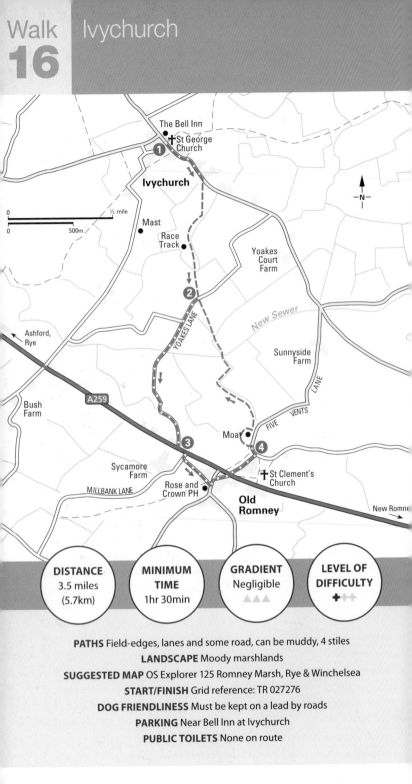

The Bell Inn
✝ St George Church
Ivychurch
1

Mast
Race Track

Yoakes Court Farm

New Sewer

2

Ashford, Rye

YOAKES LANE

Sunnyside Farm

Bush Farm

A259

VENTS LANE

Moat
4
FIVE VENTS

3

Sycamore Farm

MILLBANK LANE

Rose and Crown PH

✝ St Clement's Church

Old Romney

New Romne[y]

0   ½ mile
0   500m

—N—

DISTANCE
3.5 miles
(5.7km)

MINIMUM TIME
1hr 30min

GRADIENT
Negligible
▲▲▲

LEVEL OF DIFFICULTY
✚✚✚

PATHS Field-edges, lanes and some road, can be muddy, 4 stiles
LANDSCAPE Moody marshlands
SUGGESTED MAP OS Explorer 125 Romney Marsh, Rye & Winchelsea
START/FINISH Grid reference: TR 027276
DOG FRIENDLINESS Must be kept on a lead by roads
PARKING Near Bell Inn at Ivychurch
PUBLIC TOILETS None on route

WALK 16 DIRECTIONS

❶ With the church on your left, walk along the road, pass the phone box, then take the footpath on the right, opposite Home Farm. Go diagonally left across this field – keeping the mast on your right. If it's been raining you'll notice your boots getting weighed down with thick clay. Keep left in the next field, passing a small race track, cross two stiles and then bear diagonally right to a gate and plank bridge. Bear left, then right across the field to reach Yoakes Lane.

❷ At the track turn right and follow it all the way to Old Romney. Keep an eye out for the sight of a heron overhead. There are plenty on the marshes as they feed in the ditches that lace the ground.

🍴 EATING AND DRINKING

You're parked close to the Bell Inn in Ivychurch where you can get a drink after your walk. Or try the atmospheric Rose and Crown in Old Romney, which serves home-cooked food and a range of real ales.

❸ At Old Romney you come to the busy main road (A259), turn left and cross over into Millbank Lane, turning immediately left into Old School House Lane to follow a narrow lane to a junction at the Rose and Crown pub. Turn left, then second right and cross the A259. Take time to visit the church before continuing the walk.

⚓ ON THE WALK

In spring you might well hear a raucous croaking noise rising from the ditches in the marsh. It's the sound of the marsh frog, known locally as the 'laughing frog'. Twelve were introduced to a garden pond in 1935 and soon escaped into the surrounding marshland.

❹ Return along the track from the church to Five Vents Lane and keep ahead, soon to bear off left at a barn to walk around a curved medieval moat. Back at the road, keep left and follow the field-edge beside a ditch, crossing bridges to arrive back at Yoakes Lanes. Cross over and retrace your steps back to Ivychurch.

A CRAFTY WALK THROUGH PERRY WOOD

This circular route takes you through working woodland.

Traditional country crafts seem to have practically died out in Britain but on this walk through Perry Wood you'll see that one, the craft of coppicing, at least, is still being practised.

Coppicing is an ancient way of managing woodland. When small trees are cut down they soon send up new shoots from the base. If there is plenty of light around them they grow tall and straight – providing a supply of timber that can be used for a wide range of purposes. Different woods have different qualities. Ash, for example, absorbs shock well, so is good for making handles.

The most commonly coppiced wood today is sweet chestnut, which is highly durable and weathers to a dark grey. It is used to make fence posts, palings and hop poles. The species was introduced by the Romans, probably to provide a supply of chestnut flour for the legionaries. When blocks (or 'coups') of trees are coppiced they can go on producing wood for hundreds of years. Sweet chestnut can be harvested every 12–15 years.

Flourishing Wildlife

The beauty of coppicing is not simply that it provides timber without destroying trees. It also provides a valuable habitat for wildlife. That might sound strange but it works like this: whenever the trees are coppiced, a clear patch is created in the wood. As the sun floods in, wild flowers like bluebells, sage and foxgloves spring up. You'll also see willow herb, often known as fireweed because it loves to grow on ground that has been disturbed. These plants in turn attract insects. In time the trees begin to grow back, creating a scrubby area that is an ideal breeding ground for birds.

In chestnut coppice there is a wide range of bird species, including blackcaps, chiffchaffs, yellowhammers and nightingales. Eventually the chestnut coppice grows tall and creates a dense canopy. This is not quite as attractive to wildlife, so they move on to the next cleared area. The seeds of the plants remain dormant in the soil then spring into life when the plot is cleared again. As well as sweet chestnut, you'll see oaks, beeches and Scots pine as you wander through this working woodland.

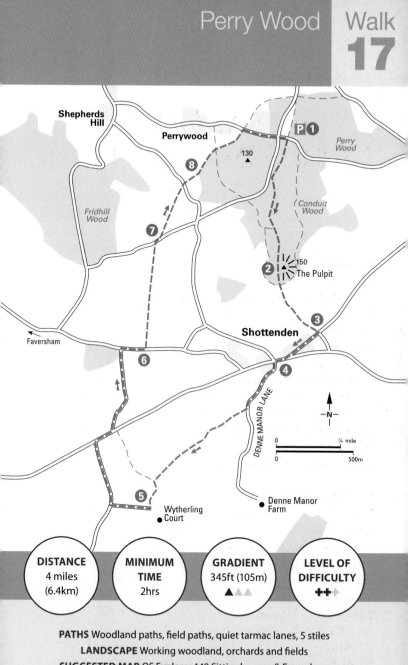

DISTANCE	MINIMUM TIME	GRADIENT	LEVEL OF DIFFICULTY
4 miles (6.4km)	2hrs	345ft (105m) ▲▲▲	++

PATHS Woodland paths, field paths, quiet tarmac lanes, 5 stiles
LANDSCAPE Working woodland, orchards and fields
SUGGESTED MAP OS Explorer 149 Sittingbourne & Faversham
START/FINISH Grid reference: TR 045556
DOG FRIENDLINESS Can mostly run free in woodland
PARKING Woodland car park in Perry Wood
PUBLIC TOILETS None on route

WALK 17 DIRECTIONS

❶ From the car park, cross the road and enter the wood, walking along the bridleway. After a few hundred paces fork left and cross the boggy ground over the boardwalk. Cross the track at Keeper's Cottage gateway and follow the bridleway steeply up, keeping right at the top, and then bear left out into open heathland. Walk along the ridge and climb to the observation platform.

❷ Walk past the picnic area, descend steeply and cross a path to enter an orchard by a stile. Continue ahead towards the bungalow at the top of the orchard. Skirt left around the garden and drop down on to the tarmac lane.

❸ Turn right to reach the centre of Shottenden, continue ahead at the junction, past the weatherboarded cottage and up to the crossroads.

❹ Turn left, signposted to Denne Manor, walk past an oast house and continue between fields. Fork right under pylons and leave the road to follow a path alongside a field. Continue along the edge of fields, your path eventually joining a farm track. Bear left to a drive at Wytherling Court.

❺ Turn right and right again at the next two T-junctions. Take the next road left, signed to Selling, to reach a T-junction. Turn right then take the waymarked footpath on the left.

❻ Your way now lies ahead across fields. Aim for the lone oak on the skyline and cross the field and a stile. Cross the next field and pasture, climbing three stiles to join the lane.

❼ Turn right along the lane, where your path soon bears left across a field towards a house. At the lane, cross to go over a field and back into the wood.

❽ Follow the path to the left and keep to the bridleway over a crossing of paths, eventually reaching a road. Turn right and go over the crossroads to reach the car park on your left.

🍴 EATING AND DRINKING

The Rose and Crown pub in Selling does a wide range of good bar meals. Alternatively you can go into Faversham where there are many pubs and coffee shops and several restaurants. Brogdale, near Faversham, also has a tearoom where you can get snacks and hot drinks.

🌿 IN THE AREA

If you're into trees you'll love Brogdale, the home of the National Fruit Collection. It's near Faversham, not far from Perry Wood and has over 2,300 varieties of apple as well as pears, cherries, plums, nuts, medlars and quinces. There are guided tours and you can buy fruit. If you've got room in the car you can even buy a tree.

A CREEKSIDE WALK FROM FAVERSHAM

A stroll to wharfs and wildlife
along the Saxon Shore Way.

If you enjoy moody marshes, a walk around Faversham Creek is definitely up your street. It isn't conventionally pretty but somehow these mournful waterlands beneath great wide skies stay in the mind's eye long after postcard scenery fades.

A ten-minute stroll along the Saxon Shore Way from the middle of one of Kent's finest historic towns leads to a scene of total solitude. On the way you'll see something of Faversham's maritime history, passing restored sailing barges and yachts moored by old wharfs and warehouses. It's a marvellous place for spotting wildlife. The marshes are alive with unusual plants and birds – take binoculars.

Old Faversham

'Bricks, beer, boots, boats and bombs' rattle off the staff at the Fleur-de-Lis Heritage Centre when you ask them what Faversham is all about. These are some of the town's former industries (the bombs referring to the gunpowder works). Sadly, most of these economic lifelines are no more, though the famous Kentish Shepherd Neame brewery has been going strong in Faversham since 1698. You can take a tour of the works on Bridge Street and sample some of its wares afterwards. The historic quarters of this enjoyable old town are crammed with Georgian and medieval buildings. The Heritage Centre, which shares premises with the tourist office in a 15th-century inn on Preston Street, is the best place to get an overview of the town's history and the trades that made it prosper. Faversham's most conspicuous church is St Mary of Charity, whose airy spire soars above the town centre. Inside it has notable monuments and misericords.

Extending the Walk

An extension to this walk leads along Oare Creek, an attractive scene of tall masts and clanking halyards fringed by reedbeds and hedges of sea buckthorn. Beyond the village of Oare over the bridge stretch more windswept marshes, now an important nature reserve for migrant birds.

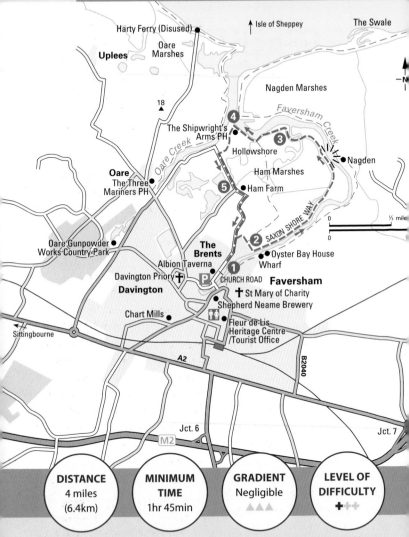

Harty Ferry (Disused)

↑ Isle of Sheppey

The Swale

Oare Marshes

Uplees

Nagden Marshes

18 ▲

Faversham Way

④

The Shipwright's Arms PH

③

Oare Creek

Hollowshore

● Nagden

Oare

The Three Mariners PH

Ham Marshes

⑤ ● Ham Farm

Faversham Creek

Oare Gunpowder Works Country Park

The Brents

Albion Taverna

Davington Priory ✝

Davington

P

① CHURCH ROAD

SAXON SHORE WAY

② ● Oyster Bay House Wharf

Faversham

✝ St Mary of Charity

Shepherd Neame Brewery

Chart Mills ●

🚻

Fleur de Lis Heritage Centre /Tourist Office

← Sittingbourne

A2

B2040

0 ½ mile

Jct. 6

M2

Jct. 7

DISTANCE	MINIMUM TIME	GRADIENT	LEVEL OF DIFFICULTY
4 miles (6.4km)	1hr 45min	Negligible ▲▲▲	✚✚✚

PATHS Raised banks through marshes; rural lanes and farm paths; several kissing gates but no stiles **LANDSCAPE** Historic wharfside, grazing marsh and creeks; lots of birdlife **SUGGESTED MAP** OS Explorer 149 Sittingbourne & Faversham **START/FINISH** Grid reference: TR 015617 **DOG FRIENDLINESS** May run free on most of the route; keep on lead near stock or on roads **PARKING** Church Road or Upper Brents (streetside or car park spaces near the Albion Taverna – check time restrictions or pay-and-display charges) **PUBLIC TOILETS** In central Faversham: at Arden Theatre car park, or Heritage Centre

WALK 18 DIRECTIONS

❶ From Front Brents car park, walk past the Albion Taverna along Faversham Creek. On the opposite bank you'll pass a gritty scene of wharfs and warehouses and modern marina-style housing, with the flying spire of St Mary of Charity visible above the rooflines. Display boards announce you are now on the Two Creeks Circular Walk. Follow the well-made path as far as you can along the waterfront, then head briefly inland, detouring around an industrial complex on your right. Follow the path along a concrete wall beside the buildings, ignoring any adjoining paths bearing off to your left. Turn right at the far end of the buildings and walk beside a couple of arable fields through a kissing gate back to the creek.

❷ Climb on to the raised bank and turn left along the Saxon Shore Way past moored boats and a handsome old warehouse (Oyster Bay House). The route is straightforward. Keeping the creek on your right, simply follow the embankment path over the marshes in a broad left-handed arc past drainage ditches, mudflats and inland lagoons. You will go through a couple of kissing gates and pass information boards with details on local wildlife etc. On the opposite bank you'll notice the odd farm at Nagden but otherwise, nothing but wildlife and views towards the Swale estuary beyond a line of pylons ahead of you.

❸ As you swing round to the left, you will pass a couple of adjoining paths on your left. Keep on the main raised track, close to the creek. Eventually a scattering of buildings appears at Hollowshore ahead, where the Faversham and Oare Creeks meet before running out to the Swale.

❹ Follow the path to the Shipwright's Arms (a wonderful place for lunch, or at least a drink). Then take the surfaced access drive from the pub past the boatyard on your right. When you reach a T-junction, turn left and follow the lane past old gravel ponds.

❺ As the road bends right, bear left up the surfaced track towards Ham Farm. Beyond the farm buildings you will pick up a footpath. Follow it as it zig-zags round field margins, first right, then left, then right again. Eventually you will find yourself back at the buildings of The Brents, where you can rejoin the Saxon Shore Way and return to your starting point.

> ⓘ **EATING AND DRINKING**
> The family-run Shipwright's Arms stands in a solitary marshland setting at Hollowshore, protected from flooding by a sea dyke. Three cosy darkwood bars full of books and boat memorabilia make this historic weatherboarded inn eternally popular with sailing folk and walkers all year round. Try the well-kept Hopdaemon or Goacher ales – Shipwrecked is a favourite.

IN THE FOOTSTEPS OF CHARING'S PILGRIMS

A gentle circuit taking you along the ancient
ridge-top track known as the Pilgrim's Way.

Charing might seem like a quaint, rather sleepy village today, but for centuries it was one of the busiest and most important settlements in Kent. It was a convenient stopping place on the medieval pilgrimage route to Canterbury and practically all pilgrims, whether rich or poor, would have stopped here for the night, before setting off the next morning for the last leg of their journey.

The Pilgrim's Way

The route known as the Pilgrim's Way in Kent, which you follow for much of this walk, was an ancient trackway used as a trading route by prehistoric people. Wherever possible it followed the top of the ridge, avoiding the thickly forested areas and sticky clay lowlands that would be so difficult to negotiate – especially in bad weather. Pilgrims wouldn't, of course, have had the benefit of modern walking boots. While the wealthy would have travelled on horseback, everyone else would have walked – generally wearing traditional pilgrim's clothes of a broad-brimmed hat and long cloak and carrying a staff and a 'scrip' – a small pouch which held necessities. Better off travellers might also have carried carved charms to protect them on their journey. Anyone undertaking the pilgrimage as a penance would probably have worn a rough, itchy 'hair shirt' as well.

While ordinary pilgrims would stay at inns along the way, bishops and archbishops expected something far grander, so archbishops' palaces were built at several points on the route. There was a particularly fine one at Charing as it was the last stopping-off point before Canterbury.

When the travellers reached the outskirts of Canterbury those on horseback would dismount and walk into the city; others would probably hobble, as no doubt their feet would have been hurting by then. After visiting the shrine of Thomas Becket in the cathedral, the pilgrims would troop off to buy badges to prove that they'd made it – rather like buying a T-shirt or car sticker today. 'Pilgrims do it on their knees', perhaps? Badges were generally decorated with a scallop shell, the symbol of St James of Compostella that is still used by pilgrims today.

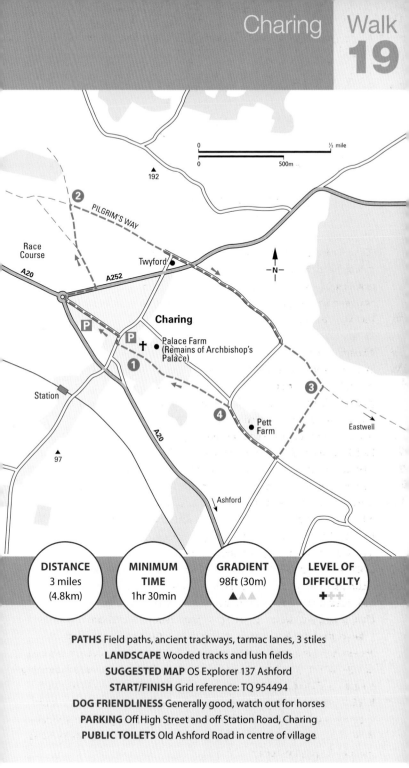

DISTANCE	MINIMUM TIME	GRADIENT	LEVEL OF DIFFICULTY
3 miles (4.8km)	1hr 30min	98ft (30m) ▲▲▲	+++

PATHS Field paths, ancient trackways, tarmac lanes, 3 stiles
LANDSCAPE Wooded tracks and lush fields
SUGGESTED MAP OS Explorer 137 Ashford
START/FINISH Grid reference: TQ 954494
DOG FRIENDLINESS Generally good, watch out for horses
PARKING Off High Street and off Station Road, Charing
PUBLIC TOILETS Old Ashford Road in centre of village

WALK 19 DIRECTIONS

❶ From the church in the centre of Charing village, walk to the High Street, cross over and go up School Road. At the roundabout turn right on to the A252 and then cross the road to follow a public footpath that leads off to the left. Go through a gate and then follow the path diagonally across a field, passing beside two metal gates. Keep to the obvious path diagonally uphill towards the trees.

❷ Pass through the hedge, cross a stile, then turn right along the Pilgrim's Way. It's easy going now, this is a popular route for dog walkers and horse riders. Continue to reach the house called Twyford. Where the track ahead forks, go to the right and come on to the A252. Cross over, turn left, walk about 50yds (46m), then turn down the Pilgrim's Way on the right-hand side. Follow the quiet tarmac lane for nearly 0.5 mile (800m) and pass a lane on your right. Continue to a lone beech tree.

> **♣ ON THE WALK**
> You can still see the flint walls of the archbishop's palace, now Palace Farm, in Charing. Henry VIII stayed here on his way to meet the king of France at the Field of the Cloth of Gold in 1520. He liked it so much that he decided to take the palace for himself at the Reformation. It was owned by the Crown until Charles II sold it. The 14th-century Great Hall is now a barn.

❸ The Pilgrims' Way now continues ahead, eventually bringing you to Eastwell, the burial place of Richard Plantaganet, illegitimate son of Richard III. Unless you want to walk to Eastwell your route now takes you to the right, down a byway. This is an immensely atmospheric lane, with a thick canopy of trees and so old that it has sunk in the middle. Take care if it's wet, as the track is chalky and can get very slippery. At the tarmac road turn right.

> **🍴 EATING AND DRINKING**
> Olivers of Charing on the High Street is a small coffee shop serving a range of drinks and decent snacks like soups, sandwiches, salads, baked potatoes and home-made cakes. It's open during the day Monday to Saturday. Alternatively, there's the Oak and Queen's Head pubs.

❹ Just past Pett Farm go over the stile by the green gate on the left-hand side. You soon see Charing church peeping through the trees. Walk towards the church, crossing another stile. At the bottom of the field, go through the hedge, cross a track and keep ahead, passing an information board for Alderbed Meadow. In a field, bear right and walk along a flagstone path and past a children's play area. Turn right up the fenced path and go into the churchyard.

PERFICK VILLAGES AROUND PLUCKLEY

A gentle ramble through the countryside
made famous by fictional Kentish family the Larkins.

There can be few such memorable fictional families as the gutsy, lusty Larkins; irrepressible Pop, voluptuous Ma, beautiful Mariette and the gaggle of noisy children. This walk takes you through the heart of *The Darling Buds of May* country, for not only was the television series filmed at Pluckley but the creator of the Larkins, H E Bates, lived at Little Chart passed on your route.

A Prolific Author

Herbert Ernest Bates was born in 1905 in Northamptonshire and moved to Little Chart in 1931 when he and his wife discovered a run-down old barn near the village. They converted it to a house, which they called The Granary, and Bates lived there until he died in 1974. Bates worked as a journalist before publishing his first book and quickly established a reputation for his stories about English country life. During the Second World War, when he served as a Squadron Leader in the RAF, he continued to write, his stories appearing under the pseudonym Flying Officer X.

The Garden of England

Bates wrote short stories, novels, plays and pieces on gardening and country life. But in everything he wrote, his love of nature shines through and in the Larkin books he brilliantly captures the beauty of the countryside around Pluckley. There are copses full of bluebells, nightingales in the woods, fields choked with strawberries and trees laden with cherries, cobnuts, pears and plums. Bates also writes of 'miles of pink apple orchards…showing petals like light confetti', and this walk takes you through the heart of some orchards. In spring you'll be able to enjoy the blossom, in autumn you'll see the apples – which, as elsewhere in Kent, often seem to be left to rot on the ground. Apple growing goes back to Roman times and the first large-scale orchards were planted for Henry VIII. Apples were highly prized and even in Victorian times ordinary people could only afford to buy windfalls and bruised fruit. Today, there are over 6,000 different varieties of apple and hundreds of types of pears, plums and cherries are grown in Kent.

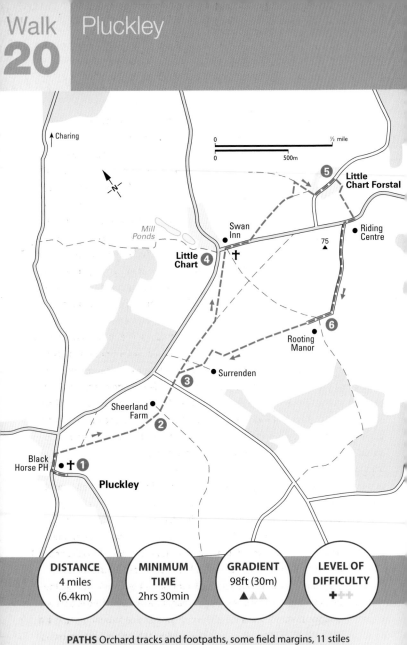

DISTANCE	MINIMUM TIME	GRADIENT	LEVEL OF DIFFICULTY
4 miles (6.4km)	2hrs 30min	98ft (30m) ▲▲▲	✚✚✚

PATHS Orchard tracks and footpaths, some field margins, 11 stiles

LANDSCAPE Apple orchards, pasture and pretty villages

SUGGESTED MAP OS Explorer 137 Ashford, Headcorn, Chilham & Wye

START/FINISH Grid reference: TQ 926453

DOG FRIENDLINESS Good but keep them on a lead

PARKING On street in Pluckley

PUBLIC TOILETS None on route

WALK 20 DIRECTIONS

❶ From the church, turn right and head up to the main road. Walk uphill, turn right by the Black Horse car park sign and make for a gate. Cut across the playing fields and through a gap in the hedge into an orchard. Carry straight on, keeping the line of trees on your right-hand side, then maintain direction to cross a metalled track by Sheerland Farm.

❷ Continue through the orchards to the road. Cross over to join a footpath by a brick wall. Follow this, climb a stile and follow the fence line on your left, to cross two more stiles at the bottom.

❸ Continue ahead, pass through a gap in a wall and enter an orchard. Follow the path ahead, cross a track and go through a gap into the next orchard. Turn left and follow the path with the windbreak on your left. Look for a gap and waymarker on the right into the adjacent orchard and continue straight on through the trees. Walk through the next orchard, enter a field and follow the grassy path ahead, with the church away to your right. Go down steps to join the road opposite the Swan Inn.

🍴 EATING AND DRINKING

The Black Horse in Pluckley serves a good range of food and real ales. The Swan Inn at Little Chart dates from the 15th century and also offers good pub food; both are open all day.

---

❹ Turn right, then cross a stile on the left beyond Laundry Cottage and head diagonally across the field – go to the left of the lone tree. Cross a stile, turn right and walk along the field-edge to cross a bridge and two stiles. Bear left, then right at the end of a garden to the road – you'll see duck ponds on either side. Follow the tarmac lane, pass a house and, at a waymarker, turn left and walk past the picture postcard village green of Little Chart Forstal.

❺ Go through the kissing gate on your right, walk down the right-hand edge of the field, cross a stile and turn left along the field-edge to a further stile to reach the road opposite the riding centre. Turn right, take the first road on the left past the farm and follow it to Rooting Manor.

❻ Where the road bends left, cross a stile by some gates, turn left, signed 'Pluckley', and walk along the top of the field. Turn right as you pass through the windbreak and walk up the orchard edge. In a few paces, take the path diagonally left and walk through the orchards and across a field to a track. Keep ahead, soon to bear left to reach Surrenden. Where the track becomes metalled, go through the kissing gate on the right and bear diagonally left across the field to a stile in the corner. Here you re-join your outward route, following the path back through orchards and past Sheerland Farm back to Pluckley.

SMARDEN'S TIMELESS CHARM

A rural ramble round a pretty Kentish weavers' village.

One of the prettiest villages in the Kentish Weald, Smarden is understandably popular. On sunny summer weekends, the village gets lots of visitors. Once away from the main streets, a wander through the lush farmland of the Beult Valley couldn't be more relaxing.

Smarden prospered on the medieval wool trade. During the reign of Edward III, skilled Flemish weavers settled in many parts of the Weald, bringing their trade secrets with them. They produced broadcloth (then the main clothing textile) and became successful enough to reverse the former trend of importing cloth from the Low Countries into a booming export trade all over Europe. Many local houses date from this era.

Period Features

If you're interested in old buildings, Smarden is a fascinating place. It's practically an illustrated textbook of vernacular architecture – a mellow assembly of half-timbering, wattle-and-daub, Kentish clapboard and tile-hung cladding. Virtually all the houses on the main street have some points of interest and several are distinctly eye-catching. The Chequers Inn dates from the 14th century, though parts are more recent. Notice the unusual curved weatherboarding at the corner of Water Lane. A few paces up is the black-and-white Old School House, bequeathed to the village by an illiterate builder in 1716 to give other poor children the chance of an education. The Dragon House opposite is a late medieval weaver's house, its gables adorned with strange carved beasts. The Cloth Hall, behind the church on Water Lane, is a striking timbered yeoman's house, while The Thatched House on the Biddenden Road played a starring role as Miss Marple's house in the film *The Mirror Crack'd* (1980).

St Michael's Church is one of Smarden's most impressive buildings. The walls consist of 'Bethersden marble', a local limestone in which you can see lots of tiny fossilised seashells. Glance inside at the fine scissor-beam roof, a cat's cradle of intersecting timbers. Almost as conspicuous are the brightly painted Gothic recesses either side of the chancel.

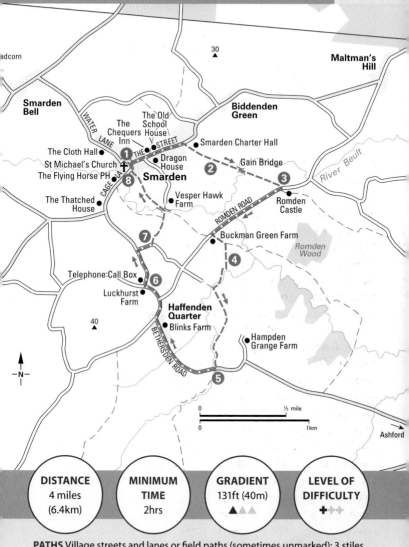

30 ▲

Maltman's Hill

Smarden Bell

WATER LANE

The Chequers Inn

The Old School House

THE STREET

Smarden Charter Hall

Biddenden Green

The Cloth Hall

St Michael's Church

The Flying Horse PH

① ②

Dragon House

Smarden

Gain Bridge

River Beult

③

CAGE LANE

⑧

Vesper Hawk Farm

Romden Castle

The Thatched House

ROMDEN ROAD

Buckman Green Farm

Romden Wood

⑦

④

Telephone Call Box

⑥

Luckhurst Farm

Haffenden Quarter

40 ▲

BETHERSDEN ROAD

Blinks Farm

Hampden Grange Farm

⑤

—N—

0 ½ mile
0 1km

Ashford

DISTANCE	MINIMUM TIME	GRADIENT	LEVEL OF DIFFICULTY
4 miles (6.4km)	2hrs	131ft (40m) ▲▲▲	+++

PATHS Village streets and lanes or field paths (sometimes unmarked); 3 stiles

LANDSCAPE Classic Kentish architecture; hop gardens, fields and water-meadows

SUGGESTED MAP OS Explorer 137 Ashford, Headcorn, Chilham & Wye

START/FINISH Grid reference: TQ 882424

DOG FRIENDLINESS May run free except on roads or near stock

PARKING Street parking in Smarden village **PUBLIC TOILETS** None on route; nearest at Headcorn **NOTE** Much of this route is very low-lying. After heavy rainfall parts could be subject to flooding

Walk 21 — Smarden

WALK 21 DIRECTIONS

1 With your back to the church, walk down Smarden's main street. At Chessenden Lane, turn right up a footpath, past the right of Smarden Charter Hall. Go through a metal kissing gate, then along the right margin of a field, past a line of oaks.

2 Take the gap through the fence and along a grassy path to a footbridge over the Beult. Keep going in the same direction through several gates until you reach Romden Road.

3 Turn right along the road, crossing a railed bridge on the way. Turn left at Buckman Green Farm, following the footpath sign. Go through a gate and down the drive past a pond. Look for a marker post and turn right across a plank footbridge.

4 At the end of the second hop garden, look for a waymarked post and turn right through a line of trees, then over a plank bridge. Walk by a stream to your left, then take wooden steps and stepping stones across a brook (take care here). Turn right along the field margin, then bear left keeping the hedge and stream to your right. Pass a path adjoining from your right; carry on here. At the next field keep ahead across the middle, heading towards the far corner (follow waymarkers to the left at the end). Follow the path, past Hampden Grange Farm, over another little plank bridge, to Bethersden Road.

5 Turn right along the road for about a mile (1.6km), passing Blinks Farm. Ignore the first two junctions and keep on the main road signed 'Smarden'.

6 At Luckhurst Farm, Bethersden Road takes a right-hand turn at another junction by a telephone box. Follow the road round a left-hand bend to the next junction and turn right at a sign for Pluckley, passing Featherstone Cottage to your right.

7 In a few paces, turn left over a waymarked stile beside a gate and cross the fields. Smarden church is visible in the distance. Make for the prominent farm buildings (Vesper Hawk Farm). As you approach its grounds, take a footbridge across a stream and turn immediately left on a grassy path past a screen of ornamental trees. At another little gate keep going across a field through a gap in the hedge ahead. Keep Smarden church ahead of you (half right). Bear slightly right towards a pole transformer and you'll see the footpath to the right of it. This leads out through a little cul-de-sac of modern housing to Cage Street by the Flying Horse.

8 Turn right and cross the road, turning through the churchyard. Then take the path to your right from the churchyard, through an archway between Providence House and West End House (an art gallery) back to The Street and the Chequers Inn.

ALONG THE PILGRIMS WAY

A breezy climb across the North Downs
following the routes of ancient trackways.

This energetic walk takes you high over the North Downs ridge, rewarding your effort with arresting views over picturesque open countryside and the attractions of a decent pub conveniently located half-way round. The whole of the Kentish Downs is classified as an Area of Outstanding Natural Beauty so there is plenty to admire along the way but you'll need good boots after rain and, be warned, there are plenty of stiles to climb.

Ancient Highways

Thanks to Chaucer, most people have heard of the Pilgrim's Way, the medieval route from London to Thomas à Becket's shrine in Canterbury. In fact, two ancient routes follow the natural causeway along the North Downs, though they don't match exactly. The pilgrims tended to walk along the southerly slopes of the ridge, avoiding too much climbing but above the beds of sticky clay coating the foot of the Downs (and their own feet too). In wet weather, you'll notice how much easier it is to walk on the chalky, flinty upper slopes, rather than the treacly stuff that turns your boots into lead weights.

Running alongside the Pilgrim's Way and sometimes converging with it, is a much older route known as the Trackway, which dates from prehistoric times. This age-old artery made use of the North Downs as a vantage point and defensive rampart. It formed part of a much larger trading route linking the Straits of Dover with the valuable mineral deposits of the West Country and the mysterious monuments at Avebury and Stonehenge.

Today, these ancient thoroughfares are partly combined in the scenic long distance trail known as the North Downs Way.

Along the Way

On the final stretch of this walk, look out for Sir Percival Pilgrim, a jovial life-size figure in medieval garb carved on a wooden bench, who creates a popular photo-opportunity for passing walkers. This merry monument is a recent project to mark the Pilgrim's Way (and reduce flytipping in the layby).

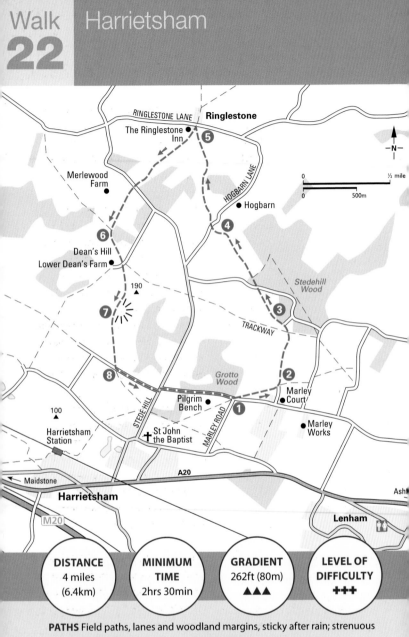

The Ringlestone Inn

Merlewood Farm

Ringlestone

RINGLESTONE LANE

HOGBARN LANE

Hogbarn

Stedehill Wood

Dean's Hill
Lower Dean's Farm

190

TRACKWAY

Grotto Wood

Marley Court

Pilgrim Bench

Marley Works

100

Harrietsham Station

St John the Baptist

MARLEY ROAD

STEDE HILL

A20

Maidstone

Harrietsham

M20

Lenham

Ash

N

0   ½ mile
0   500m

DISTANCE	MINIMUM TIME	GRADIENT	LEVEL OF DIFFICULTY
4 miles (6.4km)	2hrs 30min	262ft (80m) ▲▲▲	+++

PATHS Field paths, lanes and woodland margins, sticky after rain; strenuous gradients; 22 stiles **LANDSCAPE** Open countryside

SUGGESTED MAP OS Explorer 148 Maidstone & the Medway Towns

START/FINISH Grid reference: TQ 883534 **DOG FRIENDLINESS** May run free except near stock or on roads **PARKING** Limited roadside/layby parking along the Pilgrim's Way, by Grotto Wood. Avoid obstructing entracnces to the Marley Works (in constant use by HGVs) **PUBLIC TOILETS** None on route; nearest on Maidstone Road, off the High Street in Lenham

WALK 22 DIRECTIONS

❶ With your back to Marley Road, take the signed footpath from the Pilgrim's Way over a stile, climb steps, then head half right across a sloping field. When you reach the fenced corner of the next field, turn left towards the ridge of the North Downs, heading beneath the power lines for a gap between two buildings on the skyline.

❷ Climb the stile at the field-edge and take the steep grassy track beyond towards the farm at the brow of the hill. Turn left at the stock fence and walk along to a pair of gates. Turn right at the waymark and up the fenced path, leaving the farm buildings on your right. Bear left at a shed and follow a line of oak trees to the next stile.

❸ Continue on the track over the fields beyond, bearing diagonally half right (aim for the far corner of Stedehill Wood to your right). Take a stile into a lane. Cross and carry on past a fallen tree trunk. Make for the buildings of Hogbarn down the slope, where there are holiday chalets.

❹ Take a couple more stiles, cross Hogbarn Lane and follow the path past the farm over more stiles, bearing slightly right through a scrubby field containing caravans. Go downhill through the field, following footpath signs through a hawthorn copse, keeping a wire fence to your right. At the next field margin, bear half left again and head uphill across the next field, making for a gap in the hedge. Take more stiles until you reach the lane in Ringlestone. The Ringlestone Inn lies immediately to your left.

❺ On your return journey, take the stile back into the field from which you emerged earlier but this time turn half right, following a different footpath. Follow the waymarkers along the edges of two fields to the corner of a wood on your right, then diagonally across the next, bearing right along the margin of another wood. Cross stiles over a lane and keep straight along more field-edges, following the signs.

❻ Continue past a copse (a path adjoins from your right), bearing half left. Carry on downhill to the far corner of the field, making for the left of a line of conifers. Take a stile to your left into the lane, Dean's Hill and cross, taking the path opposite beside a 'Private Road' sign, near Lower Deans Farm.

❼ Continue diagonally half right past a white cottage to your right. Watch for signs at the end of a hedgeline on your left, bear half right and take a stile at the far hedge. Turn half left across arable fields, descending sharply.

❽ Take a stile at the far left corner of the field. Turn left and walk through trees, crossing Stede Hill. Continue on the wooded Pilgrim's Way returning to the start near Marley Road.

Leeds Castle

AROUND LEEDS CASTLE

A leisurely walk taking in handsome parkland and the setting for a thousand years of history.

Majestically moated and surrounded by beautiful grounds, Leeds Castle is a truly ethereal sight. On this walk you can see the exterior free of charge but a glance may whet your appetite to look inside. The manorial site dates back to Saxon times. The castle itself is a Norman stronghold with medieval, Tudor and Victorian additions. For 300 years the castle was a royal palace, before passing into the hands of various wealthy landowners. The influential Culpeper family owned the castle during the 17th century and a fine herb garden is one of the most interesting features of the grounds. Black swans make a dramatic sight on the castle's waterways, which were created by damming the River Len.

Leeds Castle Today

Leeds owes its present state of repair to its last private owner, the Anglo-American heiress Lady Baillie, who acquired the castle by a judicious marriage in 1926. She devoted most of her life and vast fortune to the castle's restoration. The charitable trust fund she bequeathed, along with those hefty entrance charges, ensures the castle's preservation and continued public access. Through the centuries Leeds has played host to royal and powerful visitors from all over the world but the racy interwar lives of Lady Baillie and her well-connected family are just as riveting as its history. Leeds is used for international conferences and seminars and access is occasionally restricted for security reasons.

Visitng the Castle

Leeds Castle is undoubtedly one of Kent's more expensive visitor attractions. You don't have to pay anything to enjoy this walk but this romantic place deserves a look. Your entrance ticket lasts a whole year from the date of purchase. To visit Leeds Castle, park at the main entrance and buy your ticket there. This gives you free parking and unrestricted access to the estate grounds and facilities. There is no ticket office at the castle itself. If you don't have a ticket, you must stick to the public rights of way across the estate.

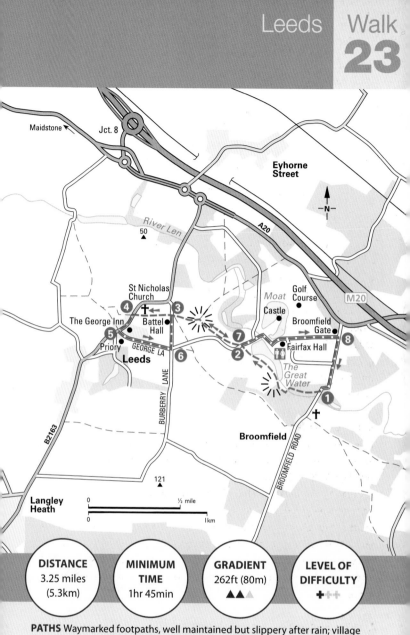

DISTANCE	MINIMUM TIME	GRADIENT	LEVEL OF DIFFICULTY
3.25 miles (5.3km)	1hr 45min	262ft (80m) ▲▲△	✚✚✚

PATHS Waymarked footpaths, well maintained but slippery after rain; village streets and country lanes, mostly without footways; no stiles

LANDSCAPE Handsome parkland **SUGGESTED MAP** OS Explorer 148 Maidstone & the Medway Towns **START/FINISH** Grid reference: TQ 841527

DOG FRIENDLINESS Dogs are not permitted within the Leeds Estate (guide dogs excepted) **PARKING** On Broomfield Road, at a wide section by the River Len (Leeds Castle car park is for paying visitors only) **PUBLIC TOILETS** None on route except at Leeds Castle (for visitors only); nearest North Street, Sutton Valence

WALK 23 DIRECTIONS

❶ A footpath runs into the Leeds Castle Estate from Broomfield Road, following the banks of the River Len. Enter the park at this point and follow the path through the woods for about 400yds (366m), before crossing the river via a footbridge. This section can get very boggy in wet weather. Bear right through the edge of the woods and go through a kissing gate into the fields beyond, continuing along the lakeshore path, with the Great Water on your right-hand side.

❷ At the far end of the lake take the path to the left of the landtrain station, heading away from the castle entrance and head uphill following the yellow waymarkers. Note – do not follow the tarmac vehicular access drive; this is not a public right of way.

❸ Follow the hill contours through sheep pasture, past a stand of trees and mini-lakes below to your right. At a converging path from the right, turn left and make for the edge of the estate, emerging on to Burberry Lane.

❹ Cross the lane and take the signed footpath opposite, crossing a field toward St Nicholas. Walk along the left-hand side of the churchyard.

❺ Go out on to the main street and turn left by the school, walking downhill past some of the older village houses for about 400yds (366m) until you reach the historic George Inn on your left. Turn left again just beyond it into George Lane.

❻ Go along to the end of George Lane (a pretty, tunnel-like walk), turning left again down Burberry Lane past a medieval house, Battel Hall, to the footpath you walked along earlier. Turn right and retrace your steps through the estate, following the yellow waymarkers. There are superb views from this section of the walk.

❼ When you reach the Great Water, turn left towards the castle island, then right before you reach the entrance bridge, taking the path between the north shore of the lake and the moat. Bear left, following the path past the castle's curtain walls to your left. Immediately to your right lies the courtyard (restaurant, museum and WCs). Continue on the blacktop path over the golf course (take care if golfers are playing), climbing gently through patches of woodland until you reach the edge of the estate at Broomfield Gate. The footpath leads to the left of the lodge gates; follow the waymarkers along a path signed '3rd Tee'. Timber steps take you out on to Broomfield Road.

❽ Turn right and walk back to your starting point just beyond a sharp double bend where the road drops steeply downhill. Be careful; there's no footway and it can be quite busy.

THE MILLS OF LOOSE

A streamside wander through the pretty Loose Valley.

Loose lies on the doorstep of the busy county town of Maidstone, yet it would be hard to imagine a more rural setting for a walk than this idyllic village. As you begin the walk, take a look to your right. The meadow on the hillside above the millpond is called Brooks Field, a popular beauty spot with a splendid view over the village. Try the 'pig-seat' at the top if you want to admire it. This piece of land was recently saved from the threat of development by a public-spirited farmer and is now maintained as an open space for the community by the parish council and local volunteers.

Unsatanic Mills

The fast-flowing river that makes such a picturesque centerpiece of both valley and village is a tributary of the Medway. Historically, it provided Loose with far more than postcard scenery. Plentiful supplies of fast-flowing, clear spring water and Fuller's earth made it a prosperous wool centre in the 16th century and a chain of watermills sprang up along the valley. When the wool trade became less profitable, the mills were converted for a new industry – paper-making, which gave an additional boost to the economy. One of the mills, Hayle Mill, is still in working order.

The Emperor's Old Clothes

The wealth of carefully preserved listed buildings in Loose indicates its former prosperity; virtually the whole village is now a conservation area. A typical example is the Wool House, a fine 17th-century timbered building on Well Street, now owned by the National Trust (not open to the public). Even older is the medieval Church of All Saints, an oddly plain structure with a shingled spire. The churchyard contains a monumental yew tree and the grave of the Reverend Richard Boys, who served as the East India Company's chaplain on the island of St Helena during Napoleon's period of exile after Waterloo. On his return to England, Boys brought with him a number of mementoes, including bits of Napoleon's uniform and a lock of his hair is now in Maidstone museum.

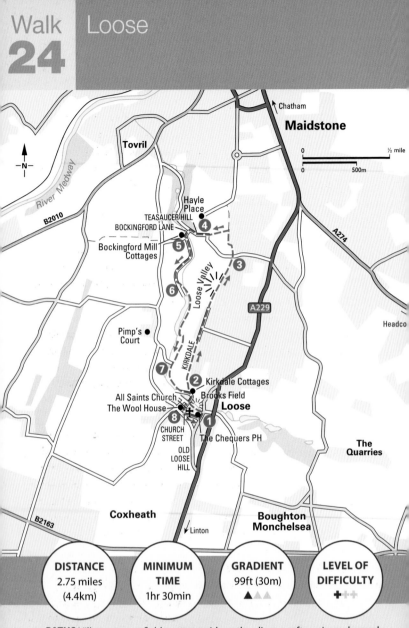

DISTANCE
2.75 miles
(4.4km)

MINIMUM TIME
1hr 30min

GRADIENT
99ft (30m)
▲▲▲

LEVEL OF DIFFICULTY
✦✦✦

PATHS Village streets; field or streamside paths, slippery after rain or churned by horses; 3 stiles **LANDSCAPE** A picturesque village and lush valley scenery beside fast-flowing water **SUGGESTED MAP** OS Explorer 148 Maidstone & the Medway Towns **START/FINISH** Grid reference: TQ 758521
DOG FRIENDLINESS May run free in places; keep under control near stock or on roads **PARKING** Streetside parking near The Chequers pub, most other streets in the village are very narrow and hilly **PUBLIC TOILETS** None on route; nearest in Maidstone

WALK 24 DIRECTIONS

❶ Take the tarmac footpath beside The Chequers pub, a raised causeway between a stream and millpond. Soon you reach a road junction (Bridge Street lies ahead of you). Take the unmade road to your right (Kirkdale), past a row of terraced cottages.

❷ Continue up this track, climbing above the waterline past woods and gardens. The path flattens out after about 200yds (183m), running straight ahead, partly on metalled surfaces, partly on grassy bridleway. Keep going past several adjoining paths. Valley views to your left become more extensive and rural.

❸ After about 0.75 miles (1.2km) cross a road (signed 'Tovil' to the left). Continue along the hedge-lined track ahead until you reach the next crossing path (a sign announces you are in the 'Loose Valley Conservation Area'). Turn left and descend on a shady path past pony paddocks and ivy-covered walls. After 150yds (137m) you reach a road at a sharp bend. A hillside house called 'Hayle Place' is signed to your right.

❹ Take the steep downhill road ahead, bearing right past restored mill houses. Turn left into Bockingford Lane and cross over the river at a stone bridge.

❺ Turn left again at a letterbox, passing Bockingford Mill Cottages on your left. Walk ahead, initially on a

flat, blacktop lane, then a waymarked footpath, keeping the river on your left. Hugging the waterfront, continue along the track beside more cottages and pastureland.

❻ Cross a stile into a glade with trees to your left. Bear slightly right, following the lower path through water-meadows past willow trees. Climb another stile and continue along the valley floor.

❼ Beyond another stile lie more fine mill buildings. Bear leftish on a broader path through a kissing gate. You will soon meet the Kirkdale path again at Kirkdale Cottages.

❽ Turn right and walk back to the road junction, taking Church Street ahead of you. Go left by the church, passing some of the older village houses. When you reach the T-junction at the top of the hill, turn left to reach your starting point by The Chequers.

🍽 EATING AND DRINKING

There's a good pub in the village, right at the start of this walk. The Chequers at Loose, as it likes to be known, is a 16th-century coaching inn in one of the village's prettiest spots, which you can enjoy from tables outside in good weather. Menus are hearty, using lots of Kentish produce and more imaginative than most – Speldhurst sausage and mash; stuffed peppers with salad.

WALKING THE WEALD AT CRANBROOK

Heritage and landscape trails around one
of Kent's most appealing towns.

The windows of Cranbrook's estate agencies show property prices stay
buoyant in this desirable little town, whatever the economic weather. And
town it is, styling itself the Capital of the Weald, though compact enough
to explore on foot. Don't miss a wander along the main streets, which are
packed with enticing shops and restaurants, as well as historic buildings.
Pick up a Heritage Trail leaflet from the helpful information centre.

Cranbrook's main landmarks are its grand church and the Union Windmill
on the other side of town. This is the tallest and finest of England's smock
mills, in full working order (worth a climb for amazing views – open summer
weekends or Wednesday afternoons). There are dozens of interesting smaller
buildings. The timbered Old Studio on the High Street served as headquarters
for the Cranbrook Colony of artists, who worked here in the late 19th century.
The Cranbrook Museum, housed in a fine 15th-century building off Carriers
Road, contains a fascinating warren of display rooms.

Cathedral of the Weald

The honey-coloured Church of St Dunstan is one of Cranbrook's greatest
treasures, occupying a raised site above the town centre. Its handsome
proportions indicate how wealthy the town was when it was constructed in
the 15th to 16th centuries. St Dunstan's is a classic example of a 'wool church',
built on the proceeds of the broadcloth industry. Outside, Old Father Time
guards the clock face with his scythe. The interior is full of interest. Look out
for the 'Green Man', a pagan figure represented in a boss on the porch ceiling
and in carved wooden shields hanging near the tower.

Sissinghurst

On the walk route, you pass close to the village of Sissinghurst and it's an easy
detour to the famous gardens of Sissinghurst Castle (National Trust) on the far
side, signed off the A262 beyond the church. Created by Vita Sackville-West
and Harold Nicholson during the 1930s, Sissinghurst is best known for its
White Garden and the Tower that Vita used for her writing.

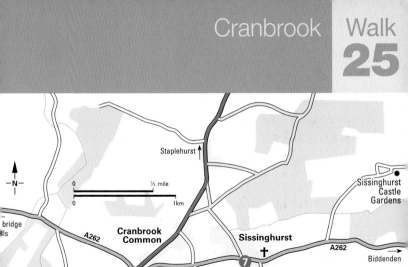

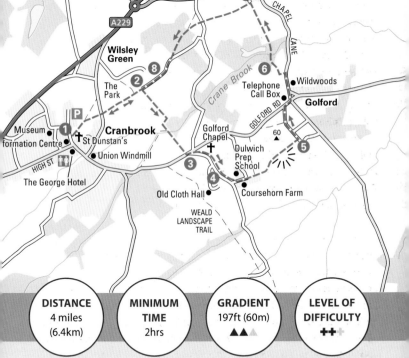

DISTANCE	MINIMUM TIME	GRADIENT	LEVEL OF DIFFICULTY
4 miles (6.4km)	2hrs	197ft (60m) ▲▲▲	++✚

PATHS Mostly well defined, sometimes surfaced field tracks or lanes; some scrambling and climbing; 2 stiles **LANDSCAPE** Woods, fields and lanes with open views of the Weald **SUGGESTED MAP** OS Explorer 136 The Weald & Royal Tunbridge Wells **START/FINISH** Grid reference: TQ 777362

DOG FRIENDLINESS May run free on much of this walk except near stock; some road walking **PARKING** There are several car parks in Cranbrook, free of charge at the time of writing. Nearest to the church is the one on Jockey Lane (off Carriers Road) **PUBLIC TOILETS** Signed from the High Street

WALK 25 DIRECTIONS

❶ From Stone Street, turn into St Dunstan's churchyard and take the paved footpath to the left of the church. Beyond it, bear half right through stone pillars, past a playground on your left. Go up the right edge of the playing fields, then down stone steps to a road. Cross over and take the footpath ahead up more steps and through a kissing gate. Continue past the landscaped grounds of The Park, fenced to your left.

❷ Shortly after passing an adjoining path from your left, turn right and turn downhill following an old hedgeline. Follow the waymarks through the wood at the bottom of the slope, briefly right, then left. Take a footbridge over Crane Brook.

❸ Following the path to the end of the trees, duck through a gap and carry on diagonally half right toward a half-timbered house. Take a kissing gate out to a road and walk left for a few paces, turning left into Cloth Hall Oast.

❹ Walk past signs for Dulwich Prep School on your left. Bear left past Coursehorn Farm, then carry on through fields , following waymarkers past a belt of trees to your left. Go through a gap at the end, then turn left over a railed ditch along a green track.

❺ Pass some oaks and houses to reach Golford Road again. Turn right for a few paces, then left into Chapel Lane at a staggered crossroads by a telephone box. Walk downhill past a house called Wildwoods on your right. Then take a stile to a footpath on your left.

❻ Head downhill through pasture (keep to the left edge if there are cattle here), then take another stile into a belt of woodland, crossing several footbridges (this bit gets quite boggy after rain). Climb a bank at the edge of the trees. Cross the hilly field beyond, heading towards buildings, then turn left at the footpath sign.

> ℹ️ **EATING AND DRINKING**
> Cranbrook has plenty of eating places. The George Hotel is a well-known central landmark dating from the 14th century. Its light, comfortable bar-lounge offers excellent coffee and pastries all day; the brasserie serves more substantial lunchtime fare.

❼ Follow a well-defined grassy track. Go down a few steep steps, crossing an adjoining byway, take a kissing gate and continue downhill through mixed woodland. Bear briefly left towards the end, take another kissing gate at the edge of the wood and meet a surfaced track converging from your left.

❽ Follow the path past Great Swifts Farm. Soon the chain-link fencing of The Park reappears on your right. Now retrace your steps past the church.

A HERBAL HIGH AROUND GOUDHURST

A short but rewarding walk around
one of Kent's highest villages.

This is the sort of walk that you can do again and again. It's varied, lovely at any time of the year and offers great views from the start – for very little effort. Even better, it's unusually well signposted – so thumbs up to the sensible farmer (or farmers) who help to keep it so enjoyable.

Traditional Medicine

Goudhurst is a very pretty village and is one of the highest villages in Kent – hence those great views. The village is dominated by St Mary's Church, which has a memorial to members of a prominent local family – the Culpepers. The family pop up all over Kent (Henry VIII's fifth wife, Catherine Howard was a Culpeper) but the most famous member was Nicholas, the physician and author of *The English Physician Enlarged,* or *The Herbal* published in 1653.

Healing Herbs

At that time the working class was moving away from the countryside and into the rapidly growing industrialised towns and cities where there were more job opportunities. In these unfamiliar, urban environments they could no longer gather the traditional herbs they used to make their own medicines. They became increasingly reliant on herbalists and apothecaries – who frequently exploited them. Nicholas Culpeper (1616–54), who trained as a herbalist in London, was conscious of the gulf between the lifestyle of his wealthy family and the majority of the population. He tried to help by letting his poor customers have their herbal medicines at low prices; always tried to use cheaper, local herbs in his remedies and would even tell people where they could go to gather the herbs themselves. He wrote his book on herbs so as to make his remedies accessible to as many people as possible. Although some of his concoctions sound rather outlandish today, many of the herbs he recommends are still in use. One of his remedies was a 'decoction' of that distinctive Kentish plant hops, which he said: 'cleanses the blood, cures the venereal disease and all kinds of scabs'. Herbalists today claim that hops are a mild sedative and contain a natural antibiotic.

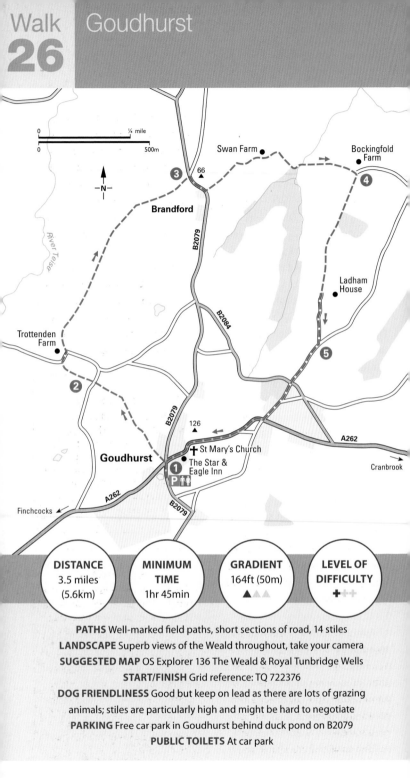

1/4 mile
500m

—N—

66 ▲

Swan Farm ●

Bockingfold Farm ●

❸

❹

Brandford

B2079

River Teise

Ladham House ●

Trottenden Farm ●

❷

B2084

❺

B2079

126 ▲

A262

✝ St Mary's Church

Goudhurst

❶ The Star & Eagle Inn

Cranbrook →

A262

B2079

← Finchcocks

DISTANCE	MINIMUM TIME	GRADIENT	LEVEL OF DIFFICULTY
3.5 miles (5.6km)	1hr 45min	164ft (50m) ▲▲▲	✚✚✚

PATHS Well-marked field paths, short sections of road, 14 stiles
LANDSCAPE Superb views of the Weald throughout, take your camera
SUGGESTED MAP OS Explorer 136 The Weald & Royal Tunbridge Wells
START/FINISH Grid reference: TQ 722376
DOG FRIENDLINESS Good but keep on lead as there are lots of grazing
animals; stiles are particularly high and might be hard to negotiate
PARKING Free car park in Goudhurst behind duck pond on B2079
PUBLIC TOILETS At car park

WALK 26 DIRECTIONS

1 Turn left uphill from the car park, pass the pond and go over a busy crossroads. Just past the bus shelter turn left and follow the waymarked High Weald Landscape Trail to a stile. Head downhill, bearing right to a stile by a tree and continue downhill crossing two fields and stiles to join an enclosed path. Climb two stiles by a pumping station, then cross a little bridge to reach a stile and road.

2 Cross over to another stile and continue ahead over pasture to a tennis court. Keep left of this to reach a stile and road. Turn right, then left in 100yds (90m), signed Trottenden Farm. In a few paces follow the drive right towards Fullers Barn and pass a pond to reach a stile. Continue ahead along a grassy track beside a fence, then cross pasture to a further stile. Follow the yellow arrows across fields and two more stiles to reach a waymarker post and a fork of paths. Turn right along the field-edge, cross a footbridge and the stile ahead on the edge of woodland. Walk uphill to another stile and follow the drive ahead to a road.

3 Turn right and at a corner turn left up a public bridleway. Bear right at Swan Cottage, then keep right at the entrance to Swan Farm and walk down into a field. At a post by a hedge turn right and go downhill. At the bottom cross some water and then veer left, walking uphill towards a farmhouse.

4 Just before the farm outbuildings turn right along a track that runs by a hedge. As you walk you will see fruit trees peeping through the gaps in the hedge. Eventually pass the parkland of Ladham House on the left and then come to some concrete bollards. Continue up the drive to join the road.

5 At the road turn right and walk up to the B2084. Cross and walk along the road in front of you. At a junction keep to the right and continue to the main road. Turn right to follow the road and walk back into the village.

🍴 EATING AND DRINKING

The ancient Star and Eagle Inn is right next to the church (a story tells that it was once connected to the church by a secret passage). It serves Sunday roasts, light meals, baguettes and teas and coffees. There are also some tea rooms and several other pubs in the village.

🌿 ON THE WALK

One local tale concerns marks on the outside of the 13th-century St Mary's Church. They are said to have been made by archers sharpening their arrows before going into battle at Agincourt in 1415. Inside the church is a brass commemorating John Bedgebury who is thought to have been one of the English knights who fought at Agincourt. There's certainly a good chance that he came to the church before heading off to war.

WHERE WATERS MEET AT YALDING

Through orchards and gardens around the Medway Valley.

Two long-distance trails meet at Yalding, the Greensand Way and the Medway Valley Walk. This walk entails a scenic stretch of the Medway and a wander through a mosaic of orchards and water-meadows south of the village. The terrain north of Yalding rises steeply to the Greensand Ridge, giving wide views across the Weald but there isn't a single contour line on this low-lying route, so it's ideal if you don't enjoy gradients. The downside is that these watery landscapes soon flood after heavy rainfall and Yalding has been inundated several times in recent years.

Yalding Village

Yalding is one of the prettiest villages on the Medway, its steep main street full of traditional Kentish houses clustered around a quaint onion-domed church. It was once an important inland port, shipping cannon down the Medway from the Wealden ironworks to the south. These days Yalding sees more leisure boating than cargo barges; moorings and marinas have sprung up around the Hampstead Lane Canal, which bypasses the medieval Twyford Bridge. The fertile greensand soils made it one of the largest hop-producers in Kent in the 1920s, though most of its thousand former hop gardens were later turned into orchards.

Three rivers converge at Yalding, so it isn't surprising to find several bridges here. Oldest is Twyford Bridge, at the confluence of the Teise and the Medway (the starting point for this walk) but the 15th-century Town Bridge across the River Beult claims to be Kent's longest medieval bridge. During the Civil War a battle took place here, won by the Roundheads.

The Yalding Gardens

These organic display gardens occupy a 5-acre (2ha) site just south of Yalding. An aerial view shows a symmetrical wheel of neatly hedged 'rooms' around a central plot. Each one has a separate theme: an apothecary's garden, an edible garden, a wildlife garden and so forth. There's a splendid on-site farm shop and café, which you can visit free of charge.

DISTANCE	MINIMUM TIME	GRADIENT	LEVEL OF DIFFICULTY
3.5 miles (5.6km)	1hr 30min	Negligible	

PATHS Riverside and field paths, muddy after rain; some road walking; 6 stiles
LANDSCAPE River valley, farmland, orchards and water-meadows
SUGGESTED MAP OS Explorer 148 Maidstone & the Medway Towns
START/FINISH Grid reference: TQ 690499 **DOG FRIENDLINESS** May run free except in private gardens or on roads; not allowed in Yalding Gardens or farmshop/café **PARKING** At Twyford Bridge or use the field car park near Teapot Island (parking charge) **PUBLIC TOILETS** In the car park by Teapot Island
NOTE Watch your step on the Medway Valley Path, it can be slippery in parts

WALK 27 DIRECTIONS

❶ Take the path between the ancient Twyford road bridge and the Anchor Inn. Cross the footbridge by the sluice gates, turning right at Teapot Island along the Medway Valley Walk. Follow the river upstream for just under a mile (1.6km). In places the path leaves the waterfront and follows a field-edge.

❷ Just before you reach the disused Stoneham Lock, look for a path to your left (if you pass the lock you've missed it). Follow the path through woodland scrub and open wasteland, bearing right, then left past old gravel workings.

❸ After about 0.75 mile (1.2km), cross a road called Gravelly Ways and take the footpath opposite past pony paddocks. Soon after crossing a concrete footbridge over the River Teise, emerge on Laddingford's main street. Turn left past The Chequers pub and walk through the village for 800yds (732m).

❹ Immediately past Laddingford House (a long, low building on your right), turn right and walk up the drive beside a brick wall, passing a cream house, Yew Tree Cottage, on your right. (Ignore the parallel section of fenced footpath to your left, which is badly overgrown.) Climb the stile ahead of you and follow the tunnel-like track, bearing left past a duck pond to your right. Weave through private gardens via stiles, a kissing gate and a footbridge over a creek, then turn left through a latch gate on to Symonds Lane.

❺ Turn right for a few paces, then left at Mill Place Farmhouse, taking a footpath across fields and orchards past a line of conifers. Follow the path along a chain-link fence to the right as far as a kissing gate leading to the main road. To your right, a short permissive path leads to the car park and café/farm shop of Yalding Gardens (recommended).

❻ On the main Benover Road, turn left towards Yalding. When you reach Congelow Cottages (by a letterbox in the wall), turn left, taking a waymarked path beneath sycamore trees. Keep right of the hedge at the end of the field. To your right are fine views of Yalding, with the Greensand Ridge in the distance.

❼ Follow the path across fields and neglected orchards for about 0.5 miles (800m), taking a rusty metal gate on to Lees Road. Cross to a gap in a railed fence opposite and swing half right across a field.

❽ Find a gap in the far hedge and follow the path out to the B2162 near Twyford Bridge. Turn left, returning to your starting point (take care if you have to cross the bridge as there is no footway and it is very narrow and busy).

EXPLORING THE NORTH KENT MARSHES

Squaring the circuit around an evocative Dickensian setting, where a nature reserve protects Britain's largest heronry.

This rectangular walk follows a quiet route from the nature reserve of Northward Hill via the tiny settlement of St Mary Hoo, partly along the long-distance Saxon Shore Way.

This spur of marsh and low sand-and-clay hills between the Thames and Medway estuaries has been settled since the Bronze Age. The Romans made the first attempts to build sea defences and drain the marshes and later it became a Saxon 'hundred'. At the eastern end of Hoo lies the Isle of Grain, a futuristic expanse of power installations and container terminals. The rest of Hoo is mainly rural, populated by wild birds and grazing stock.

For centuries, the Hoo peninsula was a lonely and inhospitable place, its waterlogged soils too saline for agriculture, the marshes infested with mosquitoes. Convict hulks anchored just offshore in the 19th century, their desperate, shackled cargoes vividly conjured up by Dickens in the opening scenes of *Great Expectations*. But the marshes also provided a haven for wildlife, which suffered when they were drained in the 20th century.

Northward Hill Nature Reserve (RSPB)

This patchwork of woods, grassland and hawthorn scrub attracts many unusual birds, including avocets, egrets and nightingales but the reserve's most distinctive species is the grey heron; over 180 pairs breed here each year. Walking trails criss-cross the reserve, with dramatic vantage points at intervals. Spring is a good time to visit, when the herons are nesting and the woods are carpeted in bluebells. But you can spot interesting birds at any time of year, especially in winter when the trees are bare.

Several paths lead into the Northward Hill RSPB reserve from High Halstow, including one from Lodge Lane near The Red Dog pub. The main car park is signed off the Cooling road about a mile (1.6km) west of High Halstow. Recent bird sightings are listed at the entrances and there are information boards around the reserve. Some of the trails are steep and muddy after rain but there are exhilarating views over the heronry and surrounding countryside (with benches if you need a rest).

EAST MALLING'S FRUITFUL TEST BEDS

A horticultural ramble around a crop-research centre.

The village of East Malling, just west of Maidstone near the busy A20/M20 corridor lies in a rapidly expanding belt of commuter housing and has not escaped modern development. But the centre is still attractive and all around is some of the most productive fruit-growing country anywhere in England. This walk is a leisurely saunter through the grounds of a leading horticultural research establishment into prosperous equestrian terrain, then back through the oldest part of the village. There are no steep climbs or tricky paths on this walk, though parts may be muddy after rain.

The East Malling Research Centre (EMR)

First set up in 1913 as an academic institution, this experimental horticultural station (not normally open to the public) now provides independent research and consultancy services for commercial growers. The fruit-growing industry is one of Kent's economic mainstays, especially important in the Maidstone area. Keen gardeners may be familiar with the many soft fruit varieties (especially raspberries) bearing the name 'Malling'. The tree rootstocks labeled with the letter M (for Malling) were all developed here – the dwarfing version M9 is now used worldwide.

In the face of fierce competition from overseas fruit producers, Kentish farmers have had to make radical changes to the way they grow fruit crops. EMR tackles problems such as plant pests and diseases, the environmental impact of climate change, food security and the identification of crop varieties. If you buy a Cox's Orange Pippin in a supermarket, you don't want to be fobbed off with some other kind of apple – genetic markers now ensure this doesn't happen.

On the Walk

At the Concept Pear Orchard, near the entrance to the research centre, notice how every twig is carefully trained to a strict preordained pattern. Pear trees are notoriously slow to bear fruit but using these new techniques, they now begin a productive life span within a couple of years of planting.

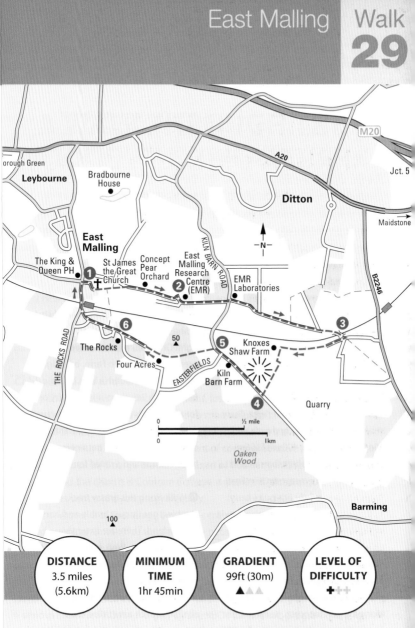

DISTANCE
3.5 miles
(5.6km)

MINIMUM TIME
1hr 45min

GRADIENT
99ft (30m)
▲▲▲

LEVEL OF DIFFICULTY
✚✚✚

PATHS Easy walking on orchard, field and railway margins; village streets or lanes; 3 stiles **LANDSCAPE** Horticultural crops and 'horsicultural' fields; historic village buildings **SUGGESTED MAP** OS Explorer 148 Maidstone & the Medway Towns **START/FINISH** Grid reference: TQ 703570

DOG FRIENDLINESS Keep under control in orchards, near animals, or on roads

PARKING On access road to St James's Church

PUBLIC TOILETS None on route, nearest at Maidstone

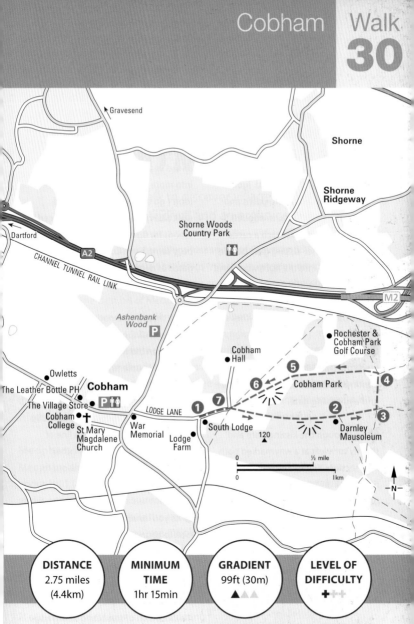

DISTANCE	MINIMUM TIME	GRADIENT	LEVEL OF DIFFICULTY
2.75 miles (4.4km)	1hr 15min	99ft (30m) ▲▲▲	✚✚✚

PATHS Mostly clear and well made, with one steep, narrow section (downhill); no stiles; several kissing gates **LANDSCAPE** Fields, wood pasture, golf course
SUGGESTED MAP OS Explorer 148 Maidstone & the Medway Towns
START/FINISH Grid reference: TQ 681684 **DOG FRIENDLINESS** Keep on lead near grazing stock or on the golf course **PARKING** At the far end of Lodge Lane, near Lodge Farm. Free parking in Cobham village too **PUBLIC TOILETS** In Cobham village car park, or at Shorne Woods Country Park visitor centre **NOTE** Cattle graze in parts of the park. Beware of low-flying golf balls while you're on the golf course

Opposite: In the grounds of St Mary Magdalene

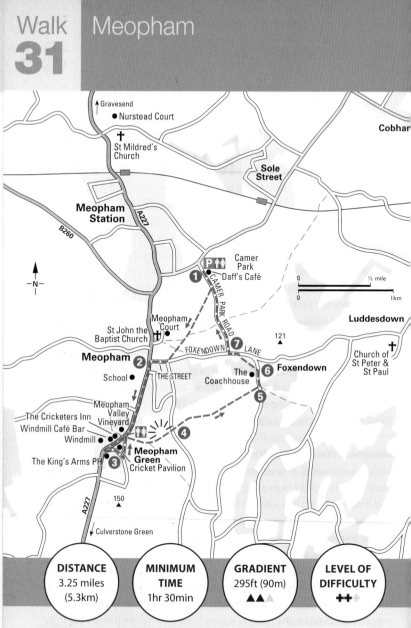

Gravesend
Nurstead Court

St Mildred's Church

Cobhar

Sole Street

Meopham Station

A227

B260

Camer Park
Daff's Café

1

CAMER PARK ROAD

Meopham Court

St John the Baptist Church

Meopham

2

School

THE STREET

FOXENDOWN LANE

7

The Coachhouse

6 Foxendown

5

121

Luddesdown

Church of St Peter & St Paul

Meopham Valley Vineyard

The Cricketers Inn

Windmill Café Bar

Windmill

The King's Arms PH

3

Meopham Green
Cricket Pavilion

4

150

Culverstone Green

–N–

0 ½ mile
0 1km

DISTANCE	MINIMUM TIME	GRADIENT	LEVEL OF DIFFICULTY
3.25 miles (5.3km)	1hr 30min	295ft (90m) ▲▲▲	++

PATHS Mostly good but steep in places and muddy after rain; some road walking, including a busy main street; no stiles; lots of kissing gates

LANDSCAPE Woods, pasture, arable fields and urban/historic village, views of the North Downs **SUGGESTED MAP** OS Explorer 148 Maidstone & the Medway Towns

START/FINISH Grid reference: TQ 650669 **DOG FRIENDLINESS** Camer Park has suggested dog walks, even a special doggy drinking tap; lead required for road walking and as requested by signs **PARKING** At Camer Park (free of charge)

PUBLIC TOILETS At Camer Park (car park), or on Meopham Green

WALK 31 DIRECTIONS

❶ Turn left from Camer Park car park and walk down the road for about 200yds (183m), then bear diagonally right at a footpath sign across a field towards a stand of ornamental trees. At the end of the field, follow the yellow waymarkers through the trees for a few paces, then go diagonally across the next field, making for a pink-washed cottage. To your right you will briefly glimpse the Gothic gables of Meopham Court among the trees and the tower of St John's Church beyond.

❷ Emerge on to The Street and turn right for 200yds (183m), then left when you reach the main road (A227). Walk through Meopham village for about 800yds (732m – the footway on the right-hand side is furthest from the traffic) passing a school, the village hall and the vineyard shop before you reach Meopham Green ahead of you. The road is quite busy, so supervise dogs and children carefully.

❸ Walk right round the green, then take the footpath signed to your right beside the Oast House (NS258). Follow it through three kissing gates before bearing diagonally left across a steep down-sloping meadow.

❹ At the bottom of the field, go through another kissing gate down wooden steps to a lane and cross over, taking the field footpath slightly to your right (look for the NS258

🍴 **EATING AND DRINKING**

Near the windmill on Meopham Green stand two attractive pubs, The Cricketers Inn and The King's Arms; both offer sophisticated bistro-style fare at lunchtimes. For something cheap and cheerful, try the Windmill Café Bar by the windmill, or Daff's Café, a kiosk snack bar at Camer Park with picnic tables outside (both serve breakfasts, bacon and sausage sandwiches, hot drinks etc).

---

marker post). Maintain your direction as before, past several buildings to either side. Make for a gap in the fence and cross a gravel drive into a long arable field flanked by belts of trees.

❺ Keep going in the same direction, following the path along the valley bottom towards the hamlet of Foxendown ahead (head for the lowest house in the dip of the vale). Take another kissing gate into the lane and turn left, climbing for 200yds (183m) past several houses.

❻ Just past The Coachhouse on your left, take the footpath to the left and climb up a fenced track between gardens and woodland, bearing right briefly at the top before emerging on to Foxendown Lane again.

❼ Turn left, then in a few paces right up Camer Park Road. The final section of the walk is an undemanding, mostly level 0.75 miles (1.2km) stretch back to Camer Park.

WITHIN FIRING RANGE OF HORSMONDEN

Through orchards and around a former gun-making centre.

Surrounded by well-tended orchards and prosperous-looking farms, it's hard to believe that Horsmonden reverberated to the din of blast furnaces and hammer forges long before the Industrial Revolution. Iron ore had been extracted in this part of the Kentish Weald since pre-Roman times, but during the 15th and 16th centuries, the smelting process became highly mechanised. Ironworks soon superseded the lucrative cloth industry as the major source of wealth and employment. Screened by trees off Furnace Lane lies a last vestige of Horsmonden's iron industry. The 30-acre (12ha) lake known as the Furnace Pond, formed by damming a small stream, once drove the giant hammers used to beat the iron into shape. It has lost its mill wheel but you can still see the spillway steps and circular basin. It is now a quiet haven for anglers and wildfowl.

Oddly, there's no parish church in the village centre; St Margaret's stands 2 miles (3.2km) away off Brick Kiln Lane, on the land of an imposing manor house. This fine sandstone church deserves a detour: several of Jane Austen's forebears are buried here and one window commemorates Simon Willard, who emigrated to Massachusetts in 1634 and founded the town of Concord.

Master of the Furnace

In the early 17th century, a local ironmaster named John Browne cornered the market in gunmaking and his foundry west of Horsmonden was soon employing 200 men to cast cannon for England's voracious munitions industry. One of his most successful lines was the Drake, a lightweight ship cannon that soon became the weapon of choice, not just for England's navy but also for many of its European colonial rivals. Charles I visited Horsmonden's famous furnace and bestowed on Browne the title of 'King's Gunfounder'. The arms trade made Browne a fortune but royal patronage didn't sway him from his Parliamentarian politics and both sides used his guns during the Civil War. By the end of the century (50 years after Browne's death), England had fought four costly battles against the Dutch, whose navy bristled with artillery forged by the great Wealden gunsmith.

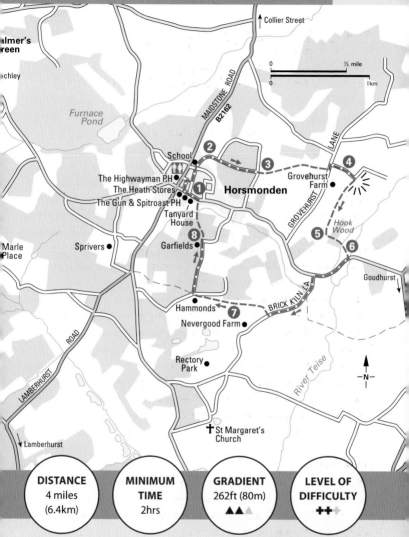

DISTANCE
4 miles
(6.4km)

MINIMUM TIME
2hrs

GRADIENT
262ft (80m)
▲▲▲

LEVEL OF DIFFICULTY
✚✚✚

PATHS Field or orchard paths, with some road walking; 8 stiles **LANDSCAPE** Fields, woods, orchards and village streets **SUGGESTED MAP** OS Explorer 136 High Weald & Royal Tunbridge Wells **START/FINISH** Grid reference: TQ 700405 **DOG FRIENDLINESS** Keep under control in orchards, near animals and on roads; some difficult stiles **PARKING** Parking around the village green **PUBLIC TOILETS** On the village green **NOTE** One section of the route is tricky to follow (some waymarkers have disappeared and trees are planted across the footpaths – look for paths or wider gaps where footpaths have been diverted)

WALK 32 DIRECTIONS

1 From the Gun & Spitroast Inn, walk up the right-hand side of the village green. At the top, take an alley next to Clock View Cottage to Back Lane. Turn left here, cross Orchard Crescent, walk ahead past the school and through a kissing gate on to a footpath.

2 Bear to the right along poplar windbreaks between orchards for about 0.75 miles (1.2km), crossing an intersecting path. Then bear half left across the next orchard, taking the waymarked path to a ditch (plank footbridge) and stile at the hedgeline.

3 Carry on down sloping pastureland into the next field, then head for the prominent buildings of Grovehurst Farm ahead of you. A fenced track and a couple of stiles take you past the farm on to Grovehurst Lane. Turn left here for a few paces, then right at a pillar box, following a footpath sign past several smart country properties.

4 Continue for 300yds (274m), turning right when you meet a crossing path at the end of the first orchard. Continue to follow the windbreak trees downhill through several orchards, turning left just beyond a hedge (following waymarkers) towards Hook Wood.

5 Halfway through this last orchard, watch carefully for a double-spaced gap in the fruit-tree lines and turn right, then left at the hedge and, in about 90 paces, cross a stile to your right. Turn left down the path through Hook Wood. Beyond a footbridge, bear slightly right across scrubland until you emerge on a metalled road. Immediately to your left is a bridge.

6 Turn right (away from the bridge) and walk for 500yds (457m). Then turn left down Brick Kiln Lane, signed 'Horsmonden Church' and carry on, weaving slightly uphill past tall hedges and banks of moss and ferns for 600yds (549m). Just past the entrance to Nevergood farmyard, take the footpath over a stile to your right, following it up the pasture to another stockfence. Cross a stile, turn left and follow the fence-line past Nevergood Farm (to your left) over another stile.

7 Now take a tunnel-like path between overgrown hedges and copses and follow it for 800yds (732m) or so over several more stiles until you reach a metalled track. A house, called Hammonds, is signed to your left. Keep ahead and in a few paces, take the lane to your right opposite Hammonds' garden gate, following it downhill for 600yds (548m) to a bungalow called 'Garfields', on your left.

8 Bear left here along a green track (leaving the metalled lane) and trickle past more orchards, over a footbridge, through a kissing gate and out on to the main village street, turning left past The Gun & Spitroast inn to the start.

TUDELEY'S GLOWING MEMORIAL

A ramble from a quiet country church illuminated by art treasures of international importance.

The bare simplicity of Tudeley's little brick-and-stone church gives little hint from outside of the glories within. But as you enter All Saints, the vivid hues of the modern windows are unexpected and visually arresting. This is Britain's largest assembly of work by the Russian-born artist Marc Chagall, a remarkable find in a country village. Chagall's stained glasswork can be seen in many other locations around the world but Tudeley is said to be the only church to have all its windows executed by the artist.

The antiquity of the church, dating back to Norman times or earlier, provides a striking foil to these 20th-century masterpieces. There's no charge to visit the church but donations are welcome to help preserve the windows.

The Chagall Windows

The windows were commissioned as a memorial to Sarah, the daughter of Sir Henry and Lady d'Avigdor-Goldsmid, who was killed in a sailing accident in 1963 aged 21 (the family lived at Somerhill, now a school, which you pass on the walk route). Initially, Chagall designed only the east window but over the next decade, the remaining 11 were installed, the final one in 1985, the year of his death. The predominant colours are blue and yellow and the subjects were inspired by Psalm 8: '*What is man that you are mindful of him...*'

In her short life, Sarah Venetia d'Avigdor-Goldsmid showed a keen eye for modern art. She bought the first picture David Hockney ever sold at a student show and had been greatly impressed by Chagall's work, which she saw on tour at the Louvre.

Tonbridge

Nearby Tonbridge has a helpful tourist office with lots of information about the local area but it's worth visiting in any case as it occupies part of the splendidly preserved gatehouse of Tonbridge Castle. The original Norman motte-and-bailey structure, predating the medieval curtain walls, remains intact. An interactive tour takes you on an entertaining journey through 700 years of history (good for children or in wet weather).

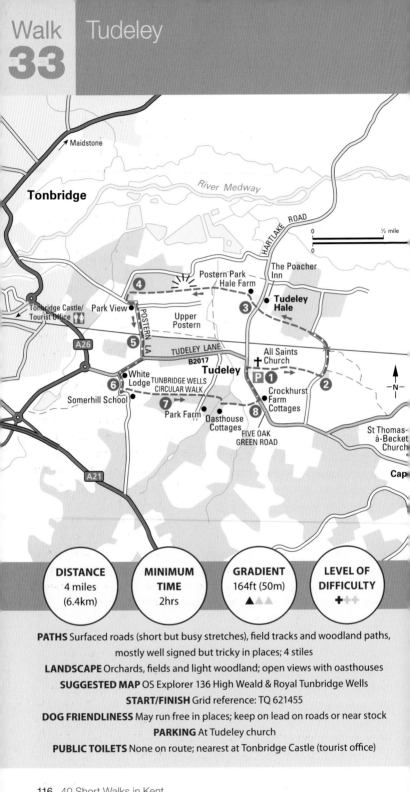

↗ Maidstone

Tonbridge

River Medway

HARTLAKE ROAD

½ mile

The Poacher Inn

Postern Park Hale Farm

4

Tonbridge Castle/ Tourist Office

Park View

POSTERN LA

Upper Postern

3

Tudeley Hale

5

TUDELEY LANE

B2017

All Saints Church

Tudeley

6

White Lodge

TUNBRIDGE WELLS CIRCULAR WALK

Somerhill School

7

Park Farm

Oasthouse Cottages

FIVE OAK GREEN ROAD

1

P

2

Crockhurst Farm Cottages

8

–N–

St Thomas- à-Becket Church

Cap

DISTANCE 4 miles (6.4km)	**MINIMUM TIME** 2hrs	**GRADIENT** 164ft (50m) ▲▲▲	**LEVEL OF DIFFICULTY** ✚✚✚

PATHS Surfaced roads (short but busy stretches), field tracks and woodland paths, mostly well signed but tricky in places; 4 stiles

LANDSCAPE Orchards, fields and light woodland; open views with oasthouses

SUGGESTED MAP OS Explorer 136 High Weald & Royal Tunbridge Wells

START/FINISH Grid reference: TQ 621455

DOG FRIENDLINESS May run free in places; keep on lead on roads or near stock

PARKING At Tudeley church

PUBLIC TOILETS None on route; nearest at Tonbridge Castle (tourist office)

WALK 33 DIRECTIONS

❶ Take the path to the far end of the churchyard, crossing a stile into a field. Walk ahead and take another stile. At the end of the field, take the kissing gate. Follow the path beside a gate, cross a stile onto the lane.

❷ Turn left, heading downhill past the farm, bearing left under the railway line. Where the lane takes a sharp right-hand bend, keep ahead on a footpath beside cottages. Carry on past orchards and fields until you emerge on Hartlake Road The Poacher Inn lies a few paces up the road to your right.

❸ Cross the road, following the signed path into a field and walk up the edge past Hale Farm (oasthouses), crossing a stile at the end. Head over another field and on through a gap in the hedgeline to more fields and orchards. Cross a footbridge, where there's an intersecting path and keep ahead.

❹ Continue following hedgelines and field margins past orchards to reach a gate into a tiny lane. Turn left here and in a few more paces turn left again into Postern Lane, following it left before turning right at Park View and passing an access road, signed 'Upper Postern'.

❺ Keep ahead along this surfaced single-track lane, through a metal gate, climbing gently to a brick-walled bridge, this time crossing high above the railway line. When you reach the B2017, turn right and walk down it for about 300yds (274m). Take care here. When the road veers right by a central reservation, cross the road and take the marked footpath beside White Lodge.

❻ In a few paces you will meet a road. Carry on up the steep hill, then turn left into the grounds of Somerhill School, taking the path to the left of the drive. Bear right at a sign 'No Unauthorised Personnel beyond this point' and follow the path beside a wall, gently downhill through woods. You are now on the Tunbridge Wells Circular Walk.

❼ Keep going through the woods and orchards, following the waymarked path. Cross a track leading to Park Farm and carry on, still heading downhill. Follow marker posts through a gap in the bank, bearing left as the drive turns right towards Oasthouse Cottages and keeping a patch of woodland on your left, carry on to the end of the field. Duck through the trees, following the waymarked path over a couple of footbridges, then keep going over the field toward a gabled house (Crockhurst Farm Cottages).

❽ The track to the left of the house leads out to Five Oak Green Road (B2017) but to avoid this busy road, take a permissive path left along the inner hedgeline. Follow the path up to the end of the field, parallel to the road, then go out on to the road, crossing to the church car park.

TASTING THE WATERS AT TUNBRIDGE WELLS

A simple trail through this elegant spa town, discovering the origins of its famous Pantiles and Royal patronage.

As you walk through the elegant streets of Tunbridge Wells, you quickly become aware that there are no medieval or Tudor buildings at all. This is because, until the 17th century, there was nothing here except thick woodland and areas of common. The town only grew up after Dudley, Lord North, whose health had been suffering from too much high living, discovered a spring while out riding in 1606. He noticed that the waters were brown and looked similar to those at a spa in Belgium. He took a drink and soon felt better (possibly feeling that if it tastes that bad it must be good for you). Word quickly spread and the great and the good started to come here to taste the waters for themselves.

Royal Patronage

The area became very popular, as it was much closer to London than other spa towns like Bath or Buxton and it soon attracted a royal visitor, Queen Henrietta Maria, Charles I's wife. As there was nowhere to stay, she and her entourage had to camp out on the common. Later visitors included Charles II, who brought both his wife and Nell Gwynne (though not necessarily at the same time), Samuel Pepys, Beau Nash and Daniel Defoe.

Gradually, lodging houses grew up around the spring, which was enclosed in the Bath House so that people could take curative baths as well as drink the waters. The area around the spring was laid out into 'walks' where people could promenade. The 'season' ran from Easter to October, when the roads from London were passable.

The Pantiles

When Queen Anne's son fell on the slippery ground she gave the town £100 so the walk could be paved with clay tiles known as pantiles. When she came back a year later she was furious to find that nothing had been done and created a regal rumpus – leading some to suggest that she was the original 'Disgusted of Tunbridge Wells'. Eventually the work was carried out and The Pantiles are still the heart of the town and have retained their elegance.

Opposite: Tunbridge Wells

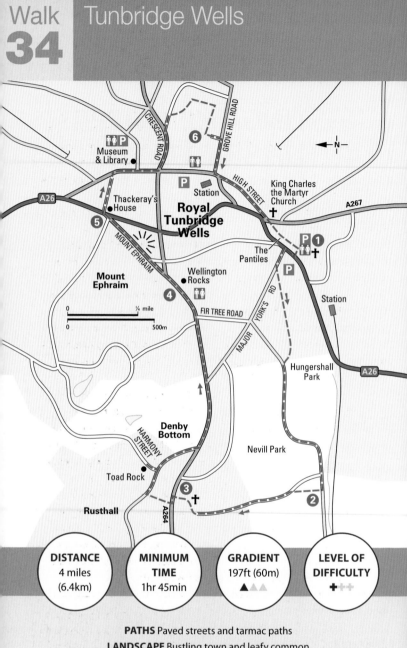

DISTANCE	MINIMUM TIME	GRADIENT	LEVEL OF DIFFICULTY
4 miles (6.4km)	1hr 45min	197ft (60m) ▲▲▲	✚✚✚

PATHS Paved streets and tarmac paths

LANDSCAPE Bustling town and leafy common

SUGGESTED MAP OS Explorer 147 Sevenoaks & Tonbridge

START/FINISH Grid reference: TQ 581386

DOG FRIENDLINESS They'll like common and rocks, otherwise it's a bit too busy

PARKING Car park behind The Pantiles or Fairground car park on Major York's Road **PUBLIC TOILETS** Pantiles, Calverley Park and town centre

WALK 34 DIRECTIONS

❶ From the car park behind The Pantiles, turn right and walk up to the main road. Cross over and then walk up Major York's Road. Just after the car park take the footpath to the left and walk across the common, keeping ahead until you reach Hungershall Park, where you turn left. Keep following the road until you come to a footpath that leads up to the right.

❷ Follow this path up through the trees which eventually leads on to a private road. Continue walking ahead and when you reach the top take the track that runs ahead through the trees. After a horse barrier, bear right to pass the churchyard, then turn right and walk around the church and up to the busy main road.

❸ Cross over, turn right for a few paces and take the footpath through the trees and across open ground to a road. Turn right, then left along Harmony Street, signed 'Toad Rock'. The road winds down to the rock (it does look rather like a toad, doesn't it?). Return to the junction, turn left then left again at the main road. Continue until you pass Fir Tree Road. On the common, hidden by the trees, are Wellington Rocks.

❹ Continue along Mount Ephraim to some cottages on the right that are built into the rock. There are seats here and you get good views over the town.

Turn right to walk across the grass and a road to the picturesque old house that was once home to the author William Makepeace Thackeray (it's unsurprisingly known as Thackeray's).

❺ Go along the path that runs by the left of the house and walk along Mount Ephraim Road. This brings you out in front of a pedestrianised shopping area. Turn right and walk down past the museum and library and the war memorial. Turn left to walk up Crescent Road and continue until you reach Calverley Park, a 19th-century housing development.

❻ Go through the entrance, then in a few paces bear left and walk across Calverley Grounds to go down Mountfield Road, then go right into Grove Hill Road. This brings you down to a roundabout where you turn left and walk along the High Street. At the end go down Chapel Place, pass the Church of King Charles the Martyr, cross the road and then walk along the famous Pantiles and back to the car park.

🍴 EATING AND DRINKING

There are lots of choices but you could try the Black Pig in Grove Hill Road for imaginative pub food; Arte Bianca, a great Italian deli in Chapel Place serving good coffee and ciabatta sandwiches; or Café Chocolat in The Pantiles, where you can sit outside and soak up the atmosphere.

HISTORY AND MYSTERY AT IGHTHAM MOTE

An easy walk to one of Kent's moated manor houses, probably one of the best examples of its kind in the country.

Unlike other counties in England, Kent has few stately homes and estates but is instead liberally scattered with farmsteads and manor houses which give the landscape a patchwork effect and add enormous variety to local walks. Yet it is only like this because, after the Norman Conquest, the people of Kent (who had a reputation for being independent and a bit aggressive) offered allegiance to William on condition that he allowed them to retain their Saxon traditions and privileges. In return they agreed to give him Dover Castle. William agreed and for centuries Kent continued to operate under its traditional administrative system.

A Hidden Treasure

Ightham Mote, which you pass on this walk, is typical of the county – a moated medieval manor house deep in the countryside, yet full of local history. The house is some distance from the village of Ightham and so well hidden that it comes as something of a surprise when you find it. Apparently, during the Civil War Cromwell's soldiers set off to loot the house but lost their way in the tangle of country lanes (Kent's signposting obviously wasn't up to much then either) and raided another house by mistake.

For hundreds of years the house was owned by the Selby family, whose most famous member was Dame Dorothy Selby. There's a memorial to her in the local church that mentions that she 'disclos'd the Plot'; seeming to imply that she foiled the Gunpowder Plot in 1605. Legend has it that she wrote an anonymous letter to her cousin, Lord Mounteagle, warning him to stay away from the opening of Parliament. He was said to have been disturbed by this and made investigations, which led to the discovery of Guy Fawkes. However, it seems more likely that Dame Dorothy, a skilled needlewoman, had simply embroidered a rather vivid picture of the Plot that people remembered.

Early in the 19th century Ightham Mote was let to an American general, William Jackson Palmer. He loved entertaining and during his time many celebrities, including Edward Burne-Jones and John Singer Sargent, Henry James and William Morris, visited the house.

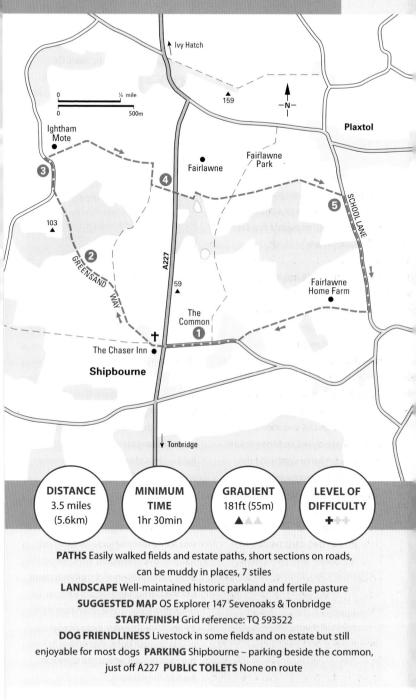

Plaxtol

Ightham
Mote

③

Fairlawne
Park

④

Fairlawne

⑤ SCHOOL LANE

103
▲

② GREENSAND WAY

A227

Fairlawne
Home Farm

59
▲

The
Common

①

✝

The Chaser Inn ●

Shipbourne

↓ Tonbridge

DISTANCE	MINIMUM TIME	GRADIENT	LEVEL OF DIFFICULTY
3.5 miles (5.6km)	1hr 30min	181ft (55m) ▲▲▲	✚✚✚

PATHS Easily walked fields and estate paths, short sections on roads, can be muddy in places, 7 stiles

LANDSCAPE Well-maintained historic parkland and fertile pasture

SUGGESTED MAP OS Explorer 147 Sevenoaks & Tonbridge

START/FINISH Grid reference: TQ 593522

DOG FRIENDLINESS Livestock in some fields and on estate but still enjoyable for most dogs **PARKING** Shipbourne – parking beside the common, just off A227 **PUBLIC TOILETS** None on route

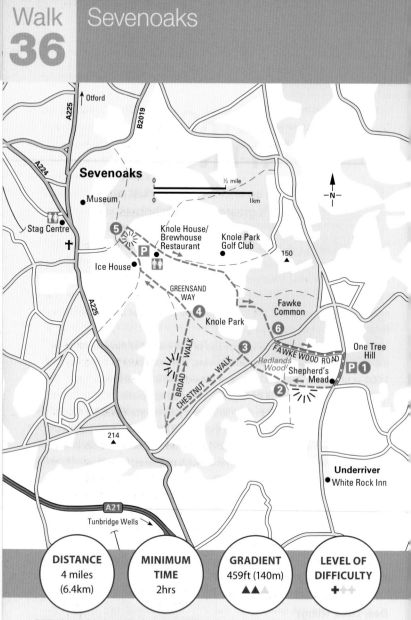

DISTANCE
4 miles (6.4km)

MINIMUM TIME
2hrs

GRADIENT
459ft (140m) ▲▲▲

LEVEL OF DIFFICULTY
✦✦✦

PATHS Mostly well-made, undulating tracks along field and woodland margins or open parkland; some sections of quiet road; 2 stiles (one need not be climbed – you can duck under a bar) **LANDSCAPE** Woods and historic parkland with herds of deer; fine Weald views **SUGGESTED MAP** OS Explorer 147 Sevenoaks & Tonbridge **START/FINISH** Grid reference: TQ 559531
DOG FRIENDLINESS Some road walking; dogs should be kept on a lead within the estate and are not allowed inside the house **PARKING** At One Tree Hill car park (free) **PUBLIC TOILETS** At Knole Park (check opening times), or in Sevenoaks

WALK 36 DIRECTIONS

❶ From the car park at One Tree Hill, turn left downhill for 200yds (183m) as far as a bend in the road and turn right on to a footpath at a house called 'Shepherd's Mead', following signs 'Greensand Way'. Walk along the edge of a belt of woodland.

❷ After about 500yds (457m) bear right at an intersecting path, then immediately left again over a stile into Redlands Field. Walk around the field margin to a stile at the far side, signed 'Greensand Way'. Take the wooded path until you reach a road (Riverhill is signed to your left). Carry on through a kissing gate in the chainlink fencing opposite into the Knole Estate.

❸ Walk ahead 100 paces until you reach the junction with the Chestnut Walk, a straight, surfaced path past an avenue of venerable trees. Turn left here and walk 0.75 miles (1.2km), then turn sharp right down the Broad Walk for a similar distance, still following Greensand Way signs.

❹ Watch carefully for a waymark post on your left just before you emerge from the trees into parkland and take this path, heading downhill. Follow the track past the house.

❺ Continue along this steep path until you reach the vehicle drive, then turn right and follow it uphill to a footpath signed on your right. This takes you over a hillock towards the car park in front of the house. Cross the car park and follow the footpath signs along the left-hand side of the house, passing the Brewhouse restaurant. At the end of the house, bear slightly left, leaving a line of beech trees on your left and following a track across the golf course. There are several paths; watch for waymarked posts and make for the left of a knoll of trees, keeping ponds on your right. You will eventually meet a track. Keep going, bearing right where the path forks, then left again past two buildings on your right. Continue to the edge of the estate and go through the gate on to the road.

❻ Cross to Fawke Wood Road, signed 'Underriver and Hildenborough'. Continue along this woodland road past several houses for about 900yds (823m). The road descends to a T-junction past a 'Slow' sign. Turn right here and within a minute you will be back at One Tree Hill car park.

🍴 EATING AND DRINKING

The Brewhouse restaurant at Knole serves sandwiches, cakes, drinks, with soup and hot dishes at lunchtimes. You can visit it without an entrance ticket but check opening hours. The nearest pub is the White Rock Inn at Underriver, which serves hot dishes, basket meals and light lunch bites most days. There's a wide choice of eating places in central Sevenoaks, from coffee shops to smart restaurants.

The magnificent gardens at Penshurst Place

THROUGH PARKLAND AT PENSHURST

A fairly easy circular walk around the magnificent estate surrounding medieval Penshurst Place.

From the very start of this walk you are rewarded with wonderful views of Penshurst Place, one of the finest medieval manor houses in England. Built in the 14th century, the house has been home to many of England's most notable and colourful characters. They include Humphrey, Duke of Gloucester (1391–1447) and brother of Henry V, who founded the Bodleian Library at Oxford; Edward Stafford, 3rd Duke of Buckingham (1478–1521), who was beheaded by Henry VIII – who then took Penshurst Place for himself; Sir William Sidney (1482–1554), who distinguished himself in battle at Flodden Field and was gifted the property by Edward VI and his descendent Algernon Sidney (c1622–1683), a Republican and supporter of Oliver Cromwell. At the Restoration Algernon was abroad and, feeling it was unsafe to return to live in England, travelled throughout Europe for many years. He eventually returned to Penshurst in order to see his dying father but he was still a marked man and was arrested on trumped up charges by Charles II and beheaded.

Local Hero

Most notable of all these residents was Sir Philip Sidney who was born here in 1554. A poet, soldier and statesman he was one of those people who seemed to do everything well. He was gifted at languages, well read, athletic, a good dancer, witty, handsome and popular. He was also, for a time, Elizabeth I's favourite courtier and she was reputedly so fond of him that she refused to let him sail to America with Sir Francis Drake – in whose work Sidney was very interested. His poetry was inspired by unrequited love – he was forbidden to marry the woman he loved – and by the countryside around Penshurst.

However, like many idols, it was only after his death that Sir Philip Sidney was established as an heroic figure. He was badly wounded fighting the Spanish and was brought some water to relieve his thirst. But he saw another wounded soldier being carried past and gave it to him instead saying 'Thy necessity is yet greater than mine'. Sidney died a few weeks later aged 32. His loss was felt so greatly that for months it was considered improper to appear at Court, or in the City, in light-coloured clothing.

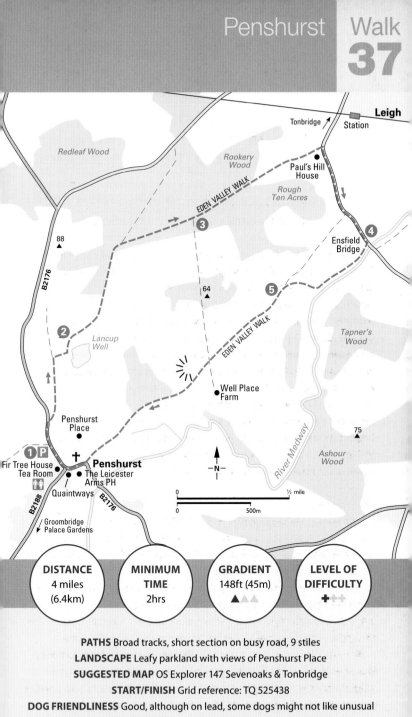

Leigh
Tonbridge
Station
Redleaf Wood
Rookery Wood
Paul's Hill House
EDEN VALLEY WALK
Rough Ten Acres
88
3
4
Ensfield Bridge
B2176
64
5
2
Lancup Well
EDEN VALLEY WALK
Tapner's Wood
Well Place Farm
75
Penshurst Place
Ashour Wood
River Medway
1 P
Fir Tree House Tea Room
Penshurst
The Leicester Arms PH
B2188
Quaintways
B2176
0   ½ mile
0   500m
–N–
Groombridge Palace Gardens

DISTANCE	MINIMUM TIME	GRADIENT	LEVEL OF DIFFICULTY
4 miles (6.4km)	2hrs	148ft (45m) ▲▲▲	+++

PATHS Broad tracks, short section on busy road, 9 stiles
LANDSCAPE Leafy parkland with views of Penshurst Place
SUGGESTED MAP OS Explorer 147 Sevenoaks & Tonbridge
START/FINISH Grid reference: TQ 525438
DOG FRIENDLINESS Good, although on lead, some dogs might not like unusual
squeeze stiles **PARKING** On-street parking in Penshurst Road,
also car park for Penshurst Place **PUBLIC TOILETS** Penshurst Road

WALK 37 DIRECTIONS

❶ Walk up the road away from the village and take the footpath right through a gate. There are great views of Penshurst Place almost immediately and it's well worth a taking a photo. The house dates from 1341 and the Great Hall is a fabulous example of medieval architecture. It has a timber roof, a musicians' gallery and an open hearth. There have been some notable visitors to the house over the years: Elizabeth I danced here with Robert Edward Dudley; the Black Prince ate a Christmas dinner here and the children of Charles I came here after their father was executed. Now bear left to another gate, cross the drive and bear slightly right across parkland, keeping lone oak trees and the lake to your right. Go through a gap in the fence and bear right to pass the lake to reach a stile.

🍴 EATING AND DRINKING

Quaintways is a lovely tea room with lots of character, in the centre of the village. They do very good cakes and scones, as well as light lunches such as sandwiches and soups. You could also try Fir Tree House Tea Rooms or The Leicester Arms.

---

❷ The path now veers to the left and goes uphill. Go through a squeeze-stile, then walk up an avenue of trees, bearing right at the top. The path levels out with good views of Penshurst Place. You are following the Eden Valley

---

🐾 ON THE WALK

In Penshurst village, look out for the 'original' Leicester Square, named after the Elizabethan Earl of Leicester. The square is enclosed by timbered and tile-hung Tudor cottages.

Walk, a 15-mile (24km) linear walk that traces the route of the Eden from Edenbridge to Tonbridge.

❸ Cross a stile and keep walking ahead along a wide, grassy track lined with trees. Exit the trees and follow the path to a stile and gate, joining a track leading down to a road beside Paul's Hill House. Turn right and follow the road (care required) to a bridge.

❹ Go through a squeeze-stile and follow the waymarked Eden Valley Walk through pasture, along the side of the River Medway which is on your left. Walk by the river for about 0.25 mile (400m), then turn right, away from the water and head across the pasture to a little bridge. Follow the footpath uphill to a stile which takes you on to a concrete track. Turn right and then left at a junction.

❺ Where the track curves sharp left, keep ahead to a stile, then bear left and walk down a path from where there are lovely views of Penshurst Place. Rejoin the concrete track and follow it under an archway, then turn right and walk back into the village.

A DARENT VALLEY WALK FROM SHOREHAM

From a delightful riverside village to hop and lavender fields and a country park.

The Darent Valley is one of Kent's prettiest areas. This walk passes through a toothsome slab of scenery around the riverside village of Shoreham, full of historic buildings and associations. One of Shoreham's highlights is its church, which has a magnificent carved rood screen, a star-spangled chancel ceiling and a Burne-Jones window. The Colgate family (of toothpaste fame) lived at Filston Hall just south of the village.

Wartime Shoreham

It's lucky that so many fine old buildings have survived. Shoreham was one of the most heavily bombed villages anywhere in Britain in the Second World War – several manor houses were requisitioned by the army and these were a target. Many local people were killed in action. A visit to Shoreham Aircraft Museum, run by volunteers from a private house in the High Street (open summer Sundays), has lots of interesting wartime stories about the area.

Above Shoreham High Street, the whitewashed cross carved in the hillside is a memorial to the casualties of the First World War. During the Second World War it was covered with earth to hide it from enemy aircraft. You will pass close by on the walk.

The Hop Shop at Castle Farm

If you come to Shoreham in high summer, you may feel you've accidentally strayed into some Provençal village. In June and July, the perfectly combed hillsides above Castle Farm erupt into a blaze of deep imperial purple when the lavender fields bloom. It is a sight – and a scent – to gladden the heart. Castle Farm is one of the UK's biggest lavender growers, producing oils and essences for culinary, cosmetic and pharmaceutical uses. You can buy the kiln-dried flowers and a host of prettily packaged lavender products at Castle Farm's on-site Hop Shop. A festival is held just before the harvest, with tours and lots of special events.

The award-winning farm shop sells lots of other local produce. It's a wonderful place to look for presents or simply a tasty cake to take home.

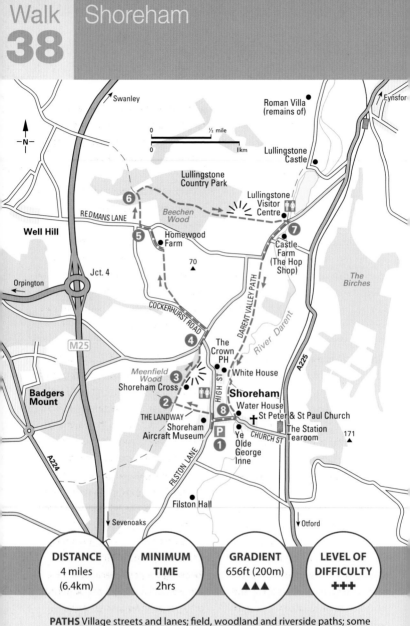

DISTANCE	MINIMUM TIME	GRADIENT	LEVEL OF DIFFICULTY
4 miles (6.4km)	2hrs	656ft (200m) ▲▲▲	+++

PATHS Village streets and lanes; field, woodland and riverside paths; some strenuous climbs; 6 stiles (not all in use; one very rickety)

LANDSCAPE Rolling fields and woods around a historic village; valley views

SUGGESTED MAP OS Explorer 147 Sevenoaks & Tonbridge

START/FINISH Grid reference: TQ 618515 **DOG FRIENDLINESS** Dogs can mostly run free on this route; some road walking **PARKING** Free car park in Shoreham (village streets are narrow and can get very congested)

PUBLIC TOILETS Shoreham village hall (seasonal) or Lullingstone Visitor Centre

WALK 38 DIRECTIONS

❶ Turn right from the Filston Lane car park and walk past the Church Street junction, along the High Street. When you reach The Landway, just past Shoreham Aircraft Museum at No 13, turn left and walk up the footpath signed 'Halstead and Timberden'. Go through a kissing gate into a field and keep ahead towards woodland. Go through a kissing gate at the field margin and climb steps through the woods until you meet a crossing path.

❷ Turn right along the woods. In 400yds (366m) reach a clearing. The Shoreham Cross memorial is below.

❸ Continue along the hillside path to the end of Meenfield Wood past a vehicle barrier and carry on across a field, losing height steadily. At the end, turn left briefly to emerge on to a lane.

❹ Turn right and downhill, bearing left past a junction to your right in a few paces. Keep going then turn left up Cockerhurst Road, signed 'Well Hill/Chelsfield'). Turn half right onto a footpath opposite a bungalow and follow the path uphill past hawthorn bushes, then bear left, following the path across fields towards Homewood Farm at the crest of the hill. Bear left at the farm, following a fence and out to Redmans Lane.

❺ Turn left here and after another 100 paces, take a rickety stile to your right and follow a footpath along a field margin, past a farm on your right, over a stile and through a metal gate into Lullingstone Country Park.

❻ Turn right at a crossing path, signed 'Visitor Centre' and keep straight ahead on the main path through mixed woodland, bearing right where the path forks (follow the black waymarkers). You reach the edge of the woods in about 0.75 miles (1.2km), then follow a track leading downhill toward Lullingstone Visitor Centre.

❼ Turn right from the visitor centre along the road, calling in at Castle Farm and the Hop Shop, reached via a little bridge to your left. Return to the road again and carry on up the hill. When the road takes a sharp right-hand bend, take the footpath to your left via a kissing gate. Keep ahead over fields, following waymarkers until you meet the River Darent at a kissing gate. Follow the river past a weir. When you emerge on to a lane, turn briefly left, then right past White House, following the path over a footbridge. Turn immediately right past waterfront cottages on the opposite bank. The river is now on your right-hand side.

❽ Follow the river until you reach Church Street by the bridge. Turn left by the bridge to the church, then retrace your steps to the T-junction at the High Street. Turn left and in a few paces you will be back at the car park.

Lavender field at sunset, Shoreham

ROYAL PASSION AT HEVER

Memories of Henry VIII and Anne Boleyn
on this circular walk.

As celebrity couples go you really can't beat the romance and tragedy of the relationship between Henry VIII and Anne Boleyn. This walk seems to remind you of them with every step, for it starts right next to Hever Castle, Anne's home and the place where the courtship took place.

A Right Royal Romance

Henry and Anne Bullen, as she was then, first met at court, where Anne was Lady-in-Waiting to the Queen, Catherine of Aragon. Anne was a sophisticated woman who had spent much of her life in France and she soon caught the eye of a young nobleman Lord Henry Percy. However, the King disapproved of the match and Anne was sent home to Hever and her father then sent her overseas. When she returned to Hever in 1525 she found that her father was swamped with honours from the King, largely as recompense for the fact that both Mary, his eldest daughter and (it was whispered) his wife had become Henry's mistresses.

Henry, desperate for a male heir and looking for a new lover, now turned his attentions to Anne, with whom he rapidly became obsessed. She was fashionable and vivacious and also had an extra finger on her left hand – which her enemies said was a sign that she was a sorceress. Henry began to visit her at Hever, turning up unannounced.

Some say Anne was ambitious and refused to become the King's mistress. Others suggest it would have been extremely difficult to repel Henry's advances. He proposed in 1527 but Anne declined – he was still married. Henry became keener and, in defiance of the Pope, divorced his wife and established the Church of England. He married Anne, who was now pregnant and she changed her name to Boleyn. She gave birth to a daughter, later to become Elizabeth I. She suffered several miscarriages and Henry, more desperate than ever for a son, became furious and claimed Anne had bewitched him. He had her imprisoned, accusing her of adultery with five men. She was found guilty of treason and beheaded on 19th May 1536. Shortly afterwards Henry married Jane Seymour, Anne's Lady-in-Waiting.

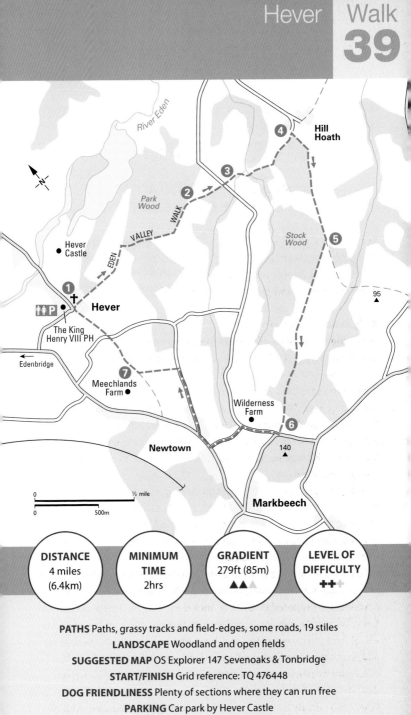

DISTANCE
4 miles
(6.4km)

MINIMUM TIME
2hrs

GRADIENT
279ft (85m)
▲▲▲

LEVEL OF DIFFICULTY
+++

PATHS Paths, grassy tracks and field-edges, some roads, 19 stiles

LANDSCAPE Woodland and open fields

SUGGESTED MAP OS Explorer 147 Sevenoaks & Tonbridge

START/FINISH Grid reference: TQ 476448

DOG FRIENDLINESS Plenty of sections where they can run free

PARKING Car park by Hever Castle

PUBLIC TOILETS At car park

WALK 39 DIRECTIONS

❶ Walk under the lychgate and go through the churchyard following the Eden Valley Walk. The path goes downhill, across a bridge and soon becomes a narrow path parallel to the road, offering occasional glimpses of the lake at Hever Castle. The path now bends round, goes through woodland, across another bridge and finally opens out.

❷ Pass beside a gate at houses, bear right and take the Eden Valley Walk to the right of Bothy Cottage. Follow the fenced path to a road.

❸ Cross over and continue along the enclosed path, which can get very muddy, crossing a stile and a footbridge. Ascend steps, join a gravel path and keep left at the junction, heading down to a gate and track at Hill Hoath.

❹ Now turn back to the right and climb the stile by the large gate, so

🌿 ON THE WALK

The magnificent gardens at Hever appear to date back to Tudor times, yet they were created at the beginning of the 20th century when William Waldorf Astor bought the castle. Astor entertained on a lavish scale and as the castle was too small to house his many guests, he built the 'Tudor' village to accommodate them.

that you seem to be doubling back on yourself. In a few paces, cross the stile on the left and follow the path uphill to a further stile. Turn left along the narrow, fenced path, which leads you into woodland.

🍴 EATING AND DRINKING

The Henry VIII pub in Hever serves food and the castle itself has tea rooms. If you're visiting the castle, and the weather's good, you could pack a picnic to eat in a quiet spot in the grounds.

❺ Keep ahead on reaching a junction of footpaths. Note that this can be exceptionally muddy. Continue down this track, passing through two areas of woodland until you come to a road.

❻ Turn right here and walk to Wilderness Farm, then take the road that leads to the left opposite the farm. At another road turn right then right again along Pigdown Lane. In 0.25 mile (400m), cross the waymarked stile on the left and go straight down the field to cross two more stiles. Bear right along the field-edge to double stiles.

❼ Continue ahead, enter the next field, passing to the left of a pond and maintain direction to a gate and road. Turn left then take the footpath on the right. Follow this back into Hever.

WALKING IN DARWIN'S FOOTSTEPS

A gentle ramble round the landscape that shaped
one of the biggest scientific ideas in history.

Downe village spans the architectural social scale from humble farm cottages
to stately Victorian mansions. In 13th-century St Mary's Church, a modern
stained-glass window to the right of the altar commemorates yachtsman and
local resident Sir Robin Knox-Johnston's lone round-the-world voyage (1968–
69). Downe Hall on Cudham Road is an imposing 19th-century house once
owned by the Lubbock family. Sir John Lubbock was a great conservationist
and friend of the Darwin family. His estate at High Elms, north-east of Downe,
is now a country park with wildlife trails and a nature centre. Rare orchids and
a thriving community of dormice inhabit its ancient woodland.

Scientific Theories at Downe

In 1842, Charles Darwin moved to Down House with his wife Emma. One
of the features that attracted them from London's bustle to the village of
Downe (then a less-than-fashionable rural backwater) was the number of
local walks: '...*almost every field is intersected by one or more footpaths. I never
saw so many walks in any other county...*' wrote Darwin to a friend. For the next
40 years, Darwin devoted his life to his expanding family and to the analysis
of a notion that shook God-fearing Victorian society to its core. He developed
his scientific theories and did his field research in and around Down House,
taking walks several times a day to clear his thoughts. Here he wrote his most
famous work *On the Origin of Species by Means of Natural Selection* (1859) and
founded the science we now call ecology.

Down House

After a chequered history in the century following Darwin's death in 1882,
Down House has been recreated by English Heritage to resemble the warm
and happy family home it was during his lifetime. Audio-tours highlight
features of the various rooms and gardens (Darwin's 'outdoor laboratory').
The Sandwalk was one of his favourite 'thinking' spots. Inside the house, you'll
find his writing desk, notebooks and a replica of the cabin where he spent five
years as a naturalist on HMS *Beagle*.

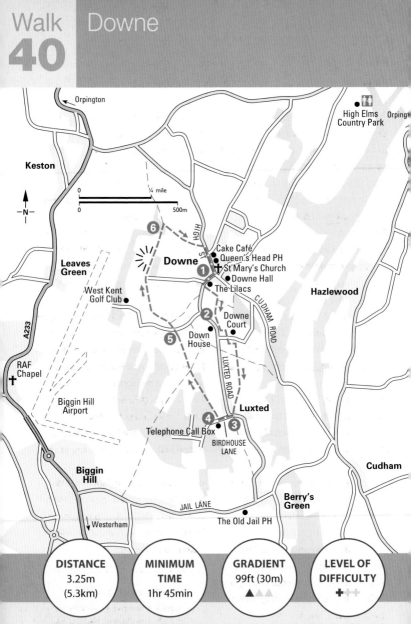

Orpington

High Elms Country Park

Orping

Keston

¼ mile

500m

—N—

6

Cake Café

Queen's Head PH

Downe St Mary's Church

1 Downe Hall

The Lilacs

Leaves Green

West Kent Golf Club

2 Downe Court

5 Down House

Hazlewood

CUDHAM ROAD

A233

RAF Chapel

Biggin Hill Airport

LUXTED ROAD

4 Luxted

3

Telephone Call Box

BIRDHOUSE LANE

Cudham

Biggin Hill

JAIL LANE

Berry's Green

The Old Jail PH

↓ Westerham

DISTANCE	MINIMUM TIME	GRADIENT	LEVEL OF DIFFICULTY
3.25m (5.3km)	1hr 45min	99ft (30m) ▲▲▲	✚✚✚

PATHS Grassy tracks, woodland paths and village streets; 6 stiles (not all in use)
LANDSCAPE Historic village, woods and quiet farmland; scenic valley views
SUGGESTED MAP OS Explorer 147 Sevenoaks & Tonbridge
START/FINISH Grid reference: TQ 432616 **DOG FRIENDLINESS** May run free in places; keep on lead on streets, in parkland or near stock; no dogs allowed at Down House. Several stiles to negotiate **PARKING** On village streets near Downe church (can be tricky in summer) **PUBLIC TOILETS** None on route; nearest at High Elms Country Park (golf clubhouse or nature centre)

WALK 40 DIRECTIONS

❶ From the church, turn left down Luxted Road, soon turning left again at a large house called 'The Lilacs' down a footpath into a field. Follow the line of tall conifers on your left, bearing briefly right at the end before taking a gap in the hedge to your left. Keep right along the next field margin, following signs for Cudham and Down House.

❷ Go through into the next field. Down House lies across a road to your right. Follow the path round the field to the far left corner and go through a kissing gate. Turn right at a waymarked post (Leaves Green Circular Walk) following more conifers. In about 50yds (46m) pass Downe Court Farmhouse. Cross a drive and carry on to a footpath marker. Turn left along the field-edge. At the end follow the field margin to the right and at the next crossing path keep ahead across fields and stiles to reach Luxted Road.

❸ Turn right along the road as far as a bend by a telephone box. Take the footpath left of the terraced cottages (Birdhouse Lane), then in 100yds (91m) turn right on to another footpath.

❹ Now head along the track past a wooded bank. Continue in the same direction for about 0.75 miles (1.2km), over a crossing footpath (follow signs ahead for Keston Common). It's a gentle uphill climb, possibly slippy after rain.

❺ At the next footpath junction near a nature reserve information board, bear left signed 'Cudham Circular Walk', then bear right around the slope for another 0.75 miles (1.2km), passing the golf clubhouse far below to your left. Go along the edge of a copse to your right, then across fields past the final stretch of the golf course. Take a kissing gate and carry on gently downhill through a grove of coppiced hazel.

❻ After 100yds (91m) take the footpath sign half right up a bank, first past a broken stile, then over another by a large oak tree and leave the trees on a path between fenced paddocks. After 200yds (183m) take a gap along a narrow fenced path beside a holly hedge towards the houses ahead. Go out on to the road beside a bus stop.

❼ Turn right past the junction with North End Lane, then rejoin the High Street towards the church tower ahead. The Cake café and The Queen's Head pub are on your left.

> 🍴 **EATING AND DRINKING**
> There are two pubs near Downe church. The Queen's Head does comforting hot dishes like home-cooked macaroni cheese. A few doors down the High Street is a café called Cake which is open most days for breakfast, light lunches and afternoon tea. Down House has tea rooms for visitors. Further afield, the Old Jail on Jail Lane, south of Luxted, is a warm and welcoming pub with good food.

Walking in Safety

All these walks are suitable for any reasonably fit person, but less experienced walkers should try the easier walks first. Route finding is usually straightforward but you will find that an Ordnance Survey map is a useful addition to the route maps and descriptions.

RISKS

Although each walk here has been researched with a view to minimising the risks to the walkers who follow its route, no walk in the countryside can be considered to be completely free from risk. Walking in the outdoors will always require a degree of common sense and judgement to ensure that it is as safe as possible.

- Be particularly careful on cliff paths and in upland terrain, where the consequences of a slip can be very serious.
- Remember to check tidal conditions before walking on the seashore.
- Some sections of route are by, or cross, busy roads. Take care and remember traffic is a danger even on minor country lanes.
- Be careful around farmyard machinery and livestock, especially if you have children with you.
- Be aware of the consequences of changes in the weather and check the forecast before you set out. Carry spare clothing and a torch if you

are walking in the winter months. Remember the weather can change very quickly at any time of the year and in moorland and heathland areas, mist and fog can make route finding much harder. Don't set out in these conditions unless you are confident of your navigation skills in poor visibility. In summer remember to take account of the heat and sun; wear a hat and carry spare water.

On walks away from centres of population you should carry a whistle and survival bag. If you do have an accident requiring the emergency services, make a note of your position as accurately as possible and dial 999.

COUNTRYSIDE CODE

- Be safe, plan ahead and follow any signs.
- Leave gates and property as you find them.
- Protect plants and animals and take your litter home.
- Keep dogs under close control.
- Consider other people.

For more information on the Countryside Code visit:
www.naturalengland.org.uk/ourwork/enjoying/countrysidecode